We are so degraded that we cannot speak simply of the necessary functions of human nature. In earlier ages, in some countries, every function was reverently spoken of and regulated by law. Nothing was too trivial for the Hindoo lawgiver, however offensive it may be to modern taste. He teaches how to eat, drink, cohabit, void excrement and urine, and the like, elevating what is mean, and does not falsely excuse himself by calling these things trifles.

Henry David Thoreau
WALDEN "Higher Laws"

Life Is Like a Chicken Coop Ladder
A Portrait of German Culture Through Folklore

*Each nation has a peculiar set of manners, and some particular qualities
are more frequently to be met with among one people than among their neighbors.*
David Hume, "Of National Characters" 1748

Photo by Bengt Holbek

LIFE IS LIKE
A CHICKEN COOP LADDER

A Portrait of German Culture Through Folklore

Alan Dundes

New York • **Columbia University Press** • *1984*

Jacket photo by A.W. Jonas

Library of Congress Cataloging in Publication Data
Dundes, Alan.
Life is like a chicken coop ladder.
Bibliography: p.
Includes index.
1. Folklore–Germany. 2. Excretion–Folklore.
3. Anus (Psychology)–Folklore. 4. Toilet training6
Germany–Folklore. 5. Feces–Folklore. 6. National
characteristics, German. I. Title.
GR166.D86 1984   398'.0943   83-7540
ISBN 0-231-05494-7
Columbia University Press
New York   Guildford, Surrey

*Clothbound editions of Columbia University Press books are Smyth-sewn
and printed on permanent and durable acid-free paper.*

CONTENTS

v

PREFACE

AN earlier version of this essay was presented in October, 1980 as the presidential address of the American Folklore Society at its annual meeting in Pittsburgh. The general response was lukewarm at best. Comments indirectly reported to me ranged from "inappropriate for after dinner" and "too long" to "an insult to members of the Society of German-American descent."

Immediately before the address was given, a group of German-born members of the Society, sitting together in the very front row and knowing the nature of the subject matter, rose and draped my shoulders with toilet paper. During the beginning of the lecture, the German group was in high spirits and good humor, and seemed to thoroughly enjoy the paper, laughing loudly and often at the various examples of folklore presented. As the argument developed and such matters as Auschwitz were discussed, there was less laughter. By the end, several of the Germans were so violently angry they were unable to speak.

In April of 1982 I had the opportunity to present an abridged version of the paper in Berlin at a conference devoted to the relationship between Volkskunde [folklore] and Völkerkunde [anthropology]. The response in Germany was more positive than that of my American colleagues. Senior scholars (mostly

German) may have disliked my argument but were too polite to say so. Their general comment (reported to me by a helpful colleague) was to the effect that they already knew about the theme but that the thesis was dismissed on the grounds that there was no such thing as national character. Younger scholars and the few students in attendance were more sympathetic, offering me numerous additional examples to buttress my conclusions. A sensitive young scholar from Tübingen told me in private "When I first read your abstract, I was very angry. Then I asked myself, why was I so angry? There must be something to the thesis after all to have caused such a strong reaction."

As should be clear from the above, this study may prove to be offensive to some readers. Even colleagues sympathetic to my research have been quick to joke about it. One has termed it a "turd de force," while another has urged that prospective readers be warned that "anyone with the vaguest interest in the subject matter cannot fail to be offended by it!" The response of a third scholar, from England, was simply that there were some things he preferred not to know. It is always difficult to investigate a taboo subject without running the risk of engendering emotion and resistance. Folklorists who work with ballads are familiar with the stylistic device called "incremental repetition" in which lines are repeated with a slight increment or addition each time. The present essay might be said to have employed a comparable technique that could perhaps be termed "excremental repetition." Yet to support the thesis proposed (and also in the interest of *ars poetica*), such repetition is probably unavoidable.

Despite the difficulties I encountered, I remain convinced that the subject of national character is an important one and that any attempt to clarify the concept is a worthwhile endeavor. I did not make up the folklore data cited in this study. The vast majority of it was readily available in the published record. The fact that no one has chosen to study the subject before is more of a comment on academic mores than on the legitimacy of the topic.

I am a folklorist with an interest in showing how folklore can be analyzed to reveal patterns of thought and worldview. I should stress that I am not a professional student of German language and culture. I have therefore elected to present many of the texts I cite in the original German, dialect spellings and all. The poetic qualities of rhyme and the cleverness of much of the word play are inevitably lost in the prosaic English translations. Since it is my hope that this research may prove of interest to readers who lack knowledge of the German language, I have attempted to provide faithful translations into English.

I wish to express my indebtedness to Dieter Rollfinke's interesting unpublished 1977 doctoral dissertation, "Menschliche Kunst: A Study of Scatology in Modern German Literature." His in-depth analysis of Wilhelm Busch, Friedrich Dürrenmatt, and Siegfried Lenz, plus other literary references to Jakov Lind and Thomas Mann, I found helpful and perceptive.

Many colleagues, friends, and students have generously offered me assistance, both in locating relevant materials and in solving problems of translation. Some of the items of folklore not specifically cited from printed sources came from some of the individuals listed below. I wish to thank them and all those who shared their expertise with me including Reinhold Aman, Florence Baer, Gunther Barth, Burton Benedict, Marianne Birnbaum, Stanley Brandes, Lisa Brinner, Felicia Browne, Pack Carnes, Elke Dettmar, James Dow, Alide Eberhard, John Fetzer,

Henry Gibbons, Nelson Graburn, Gene Hammel, Wayland Hand, Thomas Hauschild, Daniel Heartz, Ulla Johansen, Reinhard Jonas, Elliot Klein, Dorothy Koenig, Stanley Kurtz, Cornelia Levine, John Lindow, Uli Linke, Cinna Lomnitz, Leo Lowenthal, Suzanne Hoppmann-Lowenthal, James Monroe, Wolfgang Mieder, Rodney Needham, Wendy O'Flaherty, Elliot Oring, Berndt Ostendorf, Paul Rabinow, Ingrid Radke, Lutz Röhrich, Dieter Rollfinke, Hans Ruef, Elisabeth Schäfer-Wünsche, Eleonore Schamschula, Felix Scherwinsky, Eli Sobel, Margaret Sparing, Marcelo Suarez-Orozco, Robert Theodoratus, Barre Toelken, Renate Vollmer, Don Ward, Ralph Wilcoxen and Vera v. Wühlisch.

None of these people should be held responsible for errors I may have made or for my analysis of the materials they may have provided. I am aware that several of them were noticeably embarrassed by the whole project and that is why I am all the more appreciative of their kindness.

I owe a special debt to Professor Howard Stein, editor of the *Journal of Psychoanalytic Anthropology,* for publishing an earlier version of this paper in that journal in 1981. One reason for my gratitude is that the editor of the monograph series of the American Folklore Society elected not to consider the work for possible publication and decided this without even bothering to send it out for formal review.

Charles Webel, former Social Science editor of Columbia University Press, proved from the start to be enthusiastic and helpful in the magical transformation of manuscript into book. I also appreciate Leslie Bialler's conscientious and careful editorial suggestions for revision.

It is my sincere hope that anyone who takes the trouble to read this essay will find a persuasive case for the concept of national character as well as for the methodological advantages of utilizing folklore to outline the nature of the character of particular nations. My own understanding of Germany and German-speaking peoples has been irrevocably altered by the materials assembled in this study and I would like to think that most readers will also come to view Germany differently as a result of examining the same data.

For reasons which will become clearer to the reader later, I should like to dedicate this research to my great grandfather Anselm Rothschild of Heldenberger (near Frankfurt am Main), who was born January 22, 1834, came to the United States in 1852, and died in New York City on October 31, 1902.

Alan Dundes

Life Is Like a Chicken Coop Ladder
A Portrait of German Culture Through Folklore

Each nation has a peculiar set of manners, and some particular qualities
are more frequently to be met with among one people than among their neighbors.
David Hume, "Of National Characters" 1748

I INTEND to discuss a fundamental question—and I believe the answer will quite literally refer to fundament. That question is to what extent, if any, does the folklore of a given group reflect the particular character of that group? Herder claimed that the soul of a people was expressed in that people's folksongs, and others have followed with similar claims (Ergang 1931:198; Clark 1969:249). Yet despite an enormous number of writings devoted to national character, one finds few convincing demonstrations of the assertion that folklore provides an unambiguous self-portrait of a people. Folklorists have tended either to give mere lip-service to the idea or to reject the assertion uncritically, on ideological grounds.

Since so much of folklore is not confined to a single folk group, it has seemed unlikely or at least difficult to document that the folklore of a group was first of all unique or peculiar to that group and secondly that the folklore of that group contained clues to that group's personality traits. Boas, for example, published in 1935 his monograph *Kwakiutl Culture as Reflected in Mythology* in which he not only gleaned an ethnographic account of the Kwakiutl from mythological texts, but also compared the images of the Tsimshian and the Kwakiutl, two Pacific Northwest Coast Indian peoples, on the basis of

1

their respective folklore. This represented the culture-reflector approach to folklore and inherent in Boas's comparison of these two peoples was the idea of differential group identity, or in effect "national character." Yet on the whole, Boas's method of analysis tended to result in simply extrapolating ethnographic details—e.g., kinship terms, subsistence techniques, etc.—rather than defining Kwakiutl or Tsimshian personality. Similarly, Swedish folklorist von Sydow argued in favor of identifying oicotypes (1948:44-59), that is, local or regional variants of cross-cultural folklore.

Von Sydow borrowed the term oicotype from the science of botany, where it denoted a genetic variety of plant that adapted to a certain environment (e.g., seashore, mountains) through natural selection and thus differed somewhat from other members of the same species. In folklore, the term refers to local forms of a folktale, folksong or any other folkloristic genre with local defined with reference to either geographic or cultural factors. Oicotypes could be on the village, state, regional, or national level. Thus one could properly speak of a possible Swedish or Danish oicotype of a particular European ballad or folktale. If one had identified a Swedish oicotype of an international folktale, presumably one could point to distinctive Swedish features which made the tale significantly different from versions of the same folktale in other areas. But one looks in vain for extended discussion or convincing demonstrations of such oicotypes. This is unfortunate, inasmuch as the concept of oicotype is a major theoretical construct in folkloristics even though admittedly it is not widely known outside the ranks of folklorists. Even if oicotypes were delineated or identified, the question remains whether folklorists would be likely to interpret them psychologically as reflections of personality configurations.

2

It is true that anthropologists, in contrast to folklorists, frequently do tend to regard the folklore they collect in the field as unique data revealing culturally relative values, but more often than not this naive view is based upon a lack of comparative knowledge of folklore. If the same tale type is found among more than one hundred American Indian peoples, is one justified in claiming that this tale reflects special Tsimshian or Kwakiutl characteristics? I would say not without first looking at the same tale in all the cultures in which it is found. In other words, the comparative method is absolutely critical for the identification of culturally relative oicotypes. The problem historically has been that anthropologists have attempted to describe what they allege are culturally relative features without consulting the necessary (and available) comparative data, whereas folklorists have made massive comparative studies of individual customs, folktales, and the like without attempting to relate variations in these items to possible particular national penchants. A subtype of a tale type may often be found in diverse cultures and so it may be difficult to correlate its features with just one cultural context. This is why the concept of oicotype proves to be more useful than subtype for the study of national character.

It should perhaps be mentioned at the outset that the concept of national character is itself somewhat suspect. Is there in fact such a thing as national character? Or is it simply a figment of individual imaginations? Whether it exists or not, there is no question that the concept is held in low repute by European folklorists. For many European scholars, the idea of national character or "Volkscharakter" (or Volksseele, Volksgeist) remains indelibly associated with the concerted effort in Nazi Germany to use folklore as "evidence" for racial and prejudicial purposes (cf. Kamenetsky 1972, 1977). For this rea-

3

son, they eschew any attempt to study so-called national character. But this is an intellectually untenable position. The abuses of a concept should not preclude serious study of that concept. The issue of whether or not there is such a thing as national character, and if there is, whether or not it can be discovered through folklore, is a valid area of inquiry.

There is an enormous literature devoted to the subject of national character and I shall not attempt to review it here. (For representative samples of the scholarship, see Hertz 1925; Ginsberg 1942; Barker 1948; Farber 1950; Mead 1951; Brodersen 1957; Wiesbrock 1957; Nett 1958; Duijker and Frijda 1960; Maas 1960; Martindale 1967; Inkeles and Levinson 1969; Terhune 1970; Lynn 1971; Hayman 1971-1972; Favezza 1974; for a folklorist's attempt to define the concept of nationality, see van Gennep 1922.) Suffice it to say that I do not believe that national character is biological or racial in nature. Nor do I think it is geographically or climatically determined. In my view, national character is a cluster of specific personality traits which can be empirically identified. The national (or ethnic) character of people is reflected in that people's projective materials including art, music, literature, cuisine, medicine, etc. Traits or themes can be empirically observed in such projective materials. It is not just a question of an investigator postulating the existence of one or more traits which purportedly described the penchants of a particular people. The premise is rather that the trait or traits at issue are already recorded so-to-speak in the folklore of that people. Accordingly, we have only to examine the content of a people's folklore to gain access to possible clusters of personality traits. The traits may be judged positive or negative. The assessment of traits is often a relative matter. Thriftiness may be deemed admirable; stinginess deplorable, but one and the same personality trait may be

4

involved in both cases. The point is that *if* a given people does have a peculiar constellation of personality traits, those traits are likely to be expressed in a wide variety of cultural manifestations. In terms of folklore, we may find the traits articulated in folk speech, proverbs, riddles, jokes, games, and folksongs, that is, a great many folkloristic genres.

One advantage of utilizing folklore materials for the serious study of national character is precisely because the materials already exist before the investigator begins his inquiry. Too often social scientists depend upon the fabricated answers to questionnaires—often with questions based upon a *priori* assumptions held by the investigator. The folklore to be considered in this essay was not created initially as a response to the question of what is German national character? Nevertheless, it is clear that German folklore does contain numerous clues pointing to facets of German character. Also by examining data from different periods in German history, it may be demonstrated that these facets are remarkably stable over time. It would be a major enterprise to describe every single feature of the national character of any one people. The aim in the present case is much more modest. However, the same techniques employed to identify individual traits of national character could certainly be utilized to discover additional ones, among the Germans, or among other groups. Any group of people formed historically and socially for whatever reason will share common features of personality. These features will express the collective character of the group in question. Folklore provides unequalled source material for the study of features of national character.

The utilization of folklore helps solve a very vexing methodological problem concerning the crucial process of extrapolating potential national character traits from ethnographic data.

How does one select the data to be examined and how upon examination of that data does one discover possible national characteristics? Admittedly, there is always bias whenever one piece of data is adduced in lieu of another. And there is similarly the risk of bias when a researcher singles out one feature rather than another from data presented. My aim is to try to minimize the dangers of such subjective bias by using folkloristic data which I am persuaded really does display a relatively unbiased account of a people's personality or character. Folklore data, when unedited or uncensored, constitutes a kind of autobiographical ethnography, a unique way of looking at a culture from the inside-out rather than from the outside-in, the more typical situation of an outside observer trying to understand a foreign culture. If there is bias or distortion in the picture provided by folklore, at least it is produced by the people themselves and not by the would-be objective social science outsider. That is no small advantage.

Assuming that I am able to isolate any distinctive features of German national character through the evidence available in German folklore, I would be the first to admit that I would not know precisely when those features first appeared. The range of the data examined over time suggests only that the proposed pattern has existed for some centuries in what is now called Germany, but it is difficult if not impossible to establish with certainty when this pattern came into existence.

My aim is to demonstrate the configurational nature of national character. National character exists insofar as an empirically verifiable cluster of specific personality traits can be shown to be common to a particular national (or ethnic) group. If patterns of personality traits do exist, then one could reasonably surmise that such traits would be reflected in the folklore of the group in question.

Clyde Kluckhohn once wrote (1962:26) that every man is, in certain respects, (a) like all other men, (b) like some other men, and (c) like no other men. One is tempted to apply this same paradigm to nations or national character. Every nation is, in certain respects, like all other nations, like some other nations, like no other nation. It is the third possibility which is relevant to our consideration of German national character.

National character is not to be confused with national stereotypes. For one thing, the existence of national stereotypes is absolutely certain; the existence of national character continues to be debated. We know that peoples, nations, have views of themselves (self-stereotypes) and views of others (national stereotypes). Americans have stereotypes of the English, the French, the Germans, etc., just as these peoples have stereotypes of Americans. These stereotypes may be found in folklore (e.g., jokes, proverbs, folksongs) as well as in motion pictures, cartoons, novels, and the like. It is possible, and maybe even likely, that stereotypes contain a kernel of truth. Often an actual trait of national character may appear in the stereotype, although admittedly in caricature or exaggerated form.

The difficult question of the amount of overlap, if any, between national stereotypes and national character, however, is not the one I am addressing. I am more concerned at this time to demonstrate that national character exists and that its existence is unambiguously documented by the folklore of a nation. If I were pressed to distinguish national character from national stereotype, I would suggest that national character is the way people actually *are*, while national stereotypes are what people *perceive* they themselves or others are like. This raises the issue of whether we can ever progress past perception, that is, stereotypes, to get at underlying national character. It is perfectly true that many discussions of so-called national character turn out to be little more than rehashes of national stereotypes. But I believe we can define with some rigor national character and I intend to demonstrate this by examining one single trait of German character.

It is curious that the two principal objections which have been raised in response to previous attempts to delineate German national character come from extra- and intra-national concerns. On the one hand, are would-be German characteristics limited to Germany proper, or are they to be found equally among German-speaking peoples in, say, Austria and Switzerland? Are these characteristics, whatever they may be, also to be found in historically related peoples, such as the Dutch? If so, then how can one properly speak of German national character? The other objection comes from proud German regionalists who insist, not without some justification, that Prussians are "different" from Bavarians, and that Prussian character is not the same as Bavarian character. There are indisputably German regional folk cultures, each with its own sense of territorial, cultural, and often dialectal integrity (Westphalian, Hessian, Swabian, etc.) If this is the case, how can one properly speak of German national character?

I submit that there may be features—I shall be considering just one—common to all German-speaking peoples. This would not deny regional distinctions. In the same way, one can reasonably argue that there may be features common to all Americans that would similarly not deny the existence of regional distinctions in American folk cultures. That such common German characteristics might have cognate forms among other European peoples, especially those closely related historically and geographically, would not be unexpected. Thus if Dutch national character shared some features in common

8

with German national character, that would not be surprising. The point is that Germans are not the same as the French, the Italians, the Spanish, the Finns, etc. And if one admits that, then one admits the possibility of there being such a thing as national character. Lowie in *Toward Understanding Germany* stated the issue succinctly: "No trait, no attitude, is *the* German trait or attitude unless it is pan-German and pandiachronically so; and it is not distinctively German unless it is found only among Germans" (1954:354). Let us now turn to one hypothetical German character trait as a test case.

In German folklore, one finds an inordinate number of texts concerned with anality. Scheisse (shit), Dreck (dirt), Mist (manure), Arsch (ass), and similar locutions are commonplace. Folksongs, folktales, proverbs, riddles, folk speech—all attest to the Germans' longstanding special interest in this area of human activity. I am not claiming that other peoples in the world do not also express a healthy concern for this area, but rather that the Germans appear to be preoccupied with such themes. It is thus not so much a matter of difference as it is of degree. It would take far too long to list every idiomatic expression in German—either literal or metaphorical—that treats the act of defecation. I shall present some representative examples of this empirically observable tendency in German culture. I shall begin with the title of this essay as a case in point. There are in fact a number of distinct versions of this expression, at least one of which is probably known to most Germans:

> Das Leben ist wie eine Hühnerleiter—kurz und beschissen.
> Life is like a chicken (coop) ladder—short and shitty.

Sometimes the last portion follows a different beginning:

> Das Leben ist wie ein Kinderhemd—kurz und beschissen.
> Life is like a child's undershirt—short and shitty.

9

Sometimes the chicken coop formula is followed by a different response:

> Das Leben ist wie eine Hühnerleiter—Beschissen von oben bis unten.
> Life is like a chicken (coop) ladder—Shitty from top to bottom.

or

> Das Leben ist wie eine Hühnerleiter—Man kommt vor lauter Dreck nicht weiter.
> Life is like a chicken (coop) ladder—A person can't get ahead because of all the shit (in one's way).

I collected all of the above expressions during a brief trip to Frankfurt in the summer of 1979, but in a visit to Berlin in the spring of 1982, I elicited a more complete rhyming version of the chicken coop ladder definition of life, dating from the 1940s in Hamburg:

> Das Leben ist 'ne Hühnerleiter
> Life is like a chicken [coop] ladder
>
> vor lauter Dreck kommt man nicht weiter
> With so much shit, a person can't get ahead
>
> und wenn man endlich oben ist
> and when a person finally climbs up
>
> dann steckt man drin im tiefsten Mist
> Then he is stuck in the deepest manure.

In this last rhyming version, we have a play on the image of the ladder as a traditional metaphor for success. The importance of the ladder metaphor in German culture was noted by anthropologist Rhoda Metraux in the 1950s when she carried out a content analysis of contemporary German child-care literature. She observed that a prominent image associated with childhood and growth was that of "the steps (Stufen) which must be ascended to reach adulthood. . . . According to ideas to which this image is related, the child inevitably goes through stages (up steps) of growth—Each successive step must be ascended, but the child's ascent can be hindered, halted, or facilitated by training" (1955:213). The same metaphor is also explicit in the "Himmelsleiter" motif, the ladder to heaven.

These expressions are not of recent coinage. For example, a riddling question reported in 1908 is as follows (Luedecke 1908:189):

> Was ist das Leben? Eine Hühnerleiter; eine Sprosse ist stets beschissener wie die andere.
> What is life? A chicken (coop) ladder; each rung is shittier than the preceding one.

A year later (Berliner 1909:412) we find:

> Was ist das Leben? Ein Kinderhemd: es ist kurz und beschissen.
> What is life? A child's undershirt: it is short and shitty.

We find a similar folk definition of life in another modern text:

> Das Leben ist wie eine Brille—Man macht viel durch.
> Life is like a pair of spectacles—one suffers a lot.

This expression involves a double meaning. On the one hand, "Brille" refers to spectacles, but on the other hand, it refers to the round wooden frame one sits on in a toilet. "Durchmachen" means to bear or to suffer, but literally it means "making through" or "to drop." Thus life is like a toilet seat— one drops a lot through it. In a less subtle modern rhyming variant (Coturnix 1979:128), the same equation is made:

11

Das Leben wie ein Lokus ist. Man macht viel durch—oft ist es Mist.
Life is like a lavatory. One goes through a lot—often it is shit.

The fascination with feces is also evident in the following children's riddle (cf. Rühmkorf 1967:66):

Wie kommt Kuhscheisse auf das Dach?
How did the cowshit get on the roof?

The answer is:

Hat sich Kuh auf Schwanz geschissen und dann auf das Dach geschmissen.
The cow shit on its tail and then threw it up on the roof.

The initial question can also serve as a proverb commenting on a situation meaning "how did this mess come about?" Cow manure turns out to be quite a popular subject in German folk scatology. One finds other riddles, e.g., Es sieht aus wie Kuhscheisse, es riecht wie Kuhscheisse und ist doch keine Kuhscheisse (Apitzsch 1909:412). [It looks like cowshit, it smells like cowshit, yet it isn't cowshit.] The answer: Ochsenscheisse!!! [Oxen shit.]

Cow manure is equally popular in proverbial form. Je schöner die Kuh, desto grösser der Fladen. [The more beautiful the cow, the larger the cowflop.] and So genau schitt keen Kauh, dat'n Pund gifft! [No cow shits so exact that it gives just one pound even] (Förster 1912:480).

Cow manure was an integral part of German rural life. The manure pile (from cows, horses and, in olden times, humans) was found in the back or outside of the house. A German who has been absent from his country might, upon returning home,

12

joyfully smell the manure pile and refer to the aroma as "Hei-matluft" [home air]. The phrase connotes being glad to be home. One can detect here a definite positive association with cow manure.

Manure was, of course, used as fertilizer. A modern piece of folk poetry from the farm criticizes artificial synthetic fertilizers and praises the genuine article:

> Kunst is Dunst
> Pupp un Piss dat helpt gewiss.

Art (artificial fertilizer) is misty—cloudlike (that is, it is ethereal, not substantial). Feces and urine, that certainly helps. (This argues that the real stuff will help fertilize the crops properly.)

The pile of manure in front of a house (not so much in back) served as a public proclamation of wealth. For centuries, parents seeking a mate for their child would make assessments of the worth of a family under consideration on the basis of the manure pile standing in front of their farmhouse (Lowie 1954:54). The more farm animals a family owned, the greater would be the manure pile. The association of manure piles with wealth is an old one in German culture. In the 1669 novel *Simplicius Simplicissimus* by Grimmelshausen, a group of plundering soldiers decide to "tackle a house with the biggest heap of manure in front, as there the most wealthy fellows dwelt...." (Grimmelshausen 1964:190).

Mark Twain, in the account of his travels through Germany entitled *A Tramp Abroad,* published in 1880, was greatly amused by his encounter with manure piles in the Black Forest region. Speaking of a typical Black Forest house, he observed:

> "Before the ground-floor door was a huge pile of manure....All of the front half of the house from the ground up seemed to be

occupied by the people, the cows and the chickens, and all the rear half by draft animals and hay. But the chief feature, all around this house was the big heaps of manure. We became very familiar with the fertilizer in the Forest. We fell unconsciously into the habit of judging of a man's station in life by this outward and eloquent sign. Sometimes we said, "Here is a poor devil, this is manifest." When we saw a stately accumulation, we said, "Here is a banker." When we encountered a country seat surrounded by an Alpine pomp of manure, we said, "Doubtless a Duke lives here."

Twain then proceeded to outline a skeleton for a Black Forest novel in which a rich old farmer named Huss has inherited

a great wealth of manure, and by diligence has added to it. It is double-starred in Baedeker. [The farmer has a daughter Gretchen.] Paul Hoch, young neighbor, suitor for Gretchen's hand—ostensibly; he really wants the manure. Hoch has a good many cart-loads of the Black Forest currency himself, and therefore is a good catch; but he is sordid, mean, and without sentiment!....There is also Hans Schmidt, young neighbor, full of sentiment, full of poetry, loves Gretchen, Gretchen loves him. But he has no manure. Old Huss forbids him the house. His heart breaks, he goes away to die in the woods, far from the cruel world,—for he says, bitterly, "What is man, without manure?" [Six months later], Paul Hoch comes to old Huss and says, "I am at last as rich as you required—come and view the pile." Old Huss views it and says, "It is sufficient—take her and be happy"—meaning Gretchen. Two weeks later at the wedding reception, Huss's head bookkeeper enters and is scolded for not being able to balance the books. If the bookkeeper cannot locate the missing property, he must go to prison. The bookkeeper announces, "I have found it." "Where?" "In the bridegroom's pile!" Hoch is handcuffed and led away. Gretchen exclaims "Saved!" and "falls over the calf in a swoon of joy, but is caught in the arms of Hans Schmidt, who springs in at that moment." Hans explains that he "wandered in the solitude of the forest, longing for death but finding none, he fed upon roots, and in his bitterness, he dug for the bitterest, loathing the sweeter kind. "Digging, three days ago, I struck a manure mine!—a Golconda, a limitless Bonanza, of solid manure! I can buy you *all*, and have mountain ranges of manure

14

left." There is an immense sensation with "Exhibitions of specimens from the mine." Old Huss accepts the suit and the "Wedding takes place on the spot." (Clemens 1880:210-213).

Mark Twain through parody has skillfully delineated an aspect of German character.

Henry Mayhew in his detailed account of German life in the mid-nineteenth century confirms Mark Twain's impression. Mayhew speaks of the "boys and girls in the streets, with a barrow, broom, and shovel, gathering up the horse-dung for the increase of the much-prized muck-heap at the back of every dwelling" (Mayhew 1864: 2:611). It is by no means certain that all cultures encouraged the presence of manure piles adjacent to dwellings. (Once cannot help but think of the very first reference to the father of William Shakespeare in April 1552, when he was fined twelvepence for making, or failing to remove, a dungheap in front of his house on Henley Street in Stratford-on-Avon.)

An anthropologist investigating village life in Burkhards in the Vogelsberg region north of Frankfurt in the mid 1960s found that the venerable tradition continues (Nurge 1977:137): "One of the symbols of household wealth is the size of the manure pile. The manure pile stands in the front yard. Decades and centuries ago it must have been a more important symbol of the industry and wealth of a family than it is today but even today, when a family builds a new house and could put their manure heap in the back by changing floor plans and work routes, they do not; they put it in the front."

This same anthropologist discovered that it is not only animal feces which is used to fertilize fields. Human feces was used as well.

Also, it was quite a surprise to find that human wastes are used as fertilizer. That this was a practice in China is widely known, but I had never heard of it for Europe. The most common system is for the wastes from the indoor toilets to be caught in a cesspool near the manure heap and from this pumped, in the springtime, into wagon-size wooden barrels and sprayed onto the field. In Burkhards there are still outhouses and inside privies in use. I do not know if they also were cleaned periodically and the refuse used. I questioned specifically: Is human waste used on all fields. Possibly just on meadows and pastures? The answer was: No, it is used on all fields. (Nurge 1977:131)

Yet it is cow manure which occupies a place for special affection in German culture. Let anyone who doubts this read the words to a folksong collected in 1900 entitled "Der Kuhdreck" (Blümml 1908:89-90):

Frischa, warma Kuahdreck	Fresh, warm cow manure
Is Winter und Summa guat,	is good in winter and summer.
Im Winta für an Brustfleck	In winter for a vest
Im Summa für an Huat.	In summer for a hat.
Besser als unser Köchin	Better than our (female) cook
Kocht unser schwarze Kuah.	cooks our black cow.
Sie schmelzt uns die Pasteten	She shits us pot pies
Und den Spinat dazua.	And spinach with it.
Wann da Baua's Zwicka hat,	When the peasant has a pain,
So tuat's da Kuahdreck a,	He can cure it with cow manure.
Er tuat eahma in an Fetzn	He puts it in a rag
Und bindt eahma warm am Bau.	and bandages it warm on his belly.
Hiaz bin i von den Kuahdreck	Now I am so hoarse and completely
So heisari und ganz müad,	tired of cow manure,
I scheiss enk auf den Kuahdreck	I shit right on cow manure
und auf das ganze Liad.	and on the whole song.

Of course, it is not just cow manure which is featured in German culture. The word "Scheiss" normally refers to human feces. The author of a 1971 book entitled *The Germans* reported that an Evangelical pastor in Nurnberg told him that "Scheiss" is "the most often used word in Germany today" (Schalk 1971:40, 492). In similar fashion, a survey of literary uses of obscenity calls "Scheiss" "perhaps the most common vulgarism in German" (Witte 1975:368). Ernest Borneman in his superbly comprehensive *Sex im Volksmund* (1971:35.22) claims that no other European people uses the number of anal erotic terms in their slang as the Germans do. It should be made clear that these terms are not necessarily construed as obscene. Keith Spalding who has spent more than thirty years compiling a valuable dictionary of German figurative speech remarks in his discussion of "bescheissen" [to beshit] that the word is not normally considered vulgar when used in dialects. In fact, in dialect it is generally regarded as permissible usage. But when the idiom is used in 'proper' German, it is often considered to be a vulgarism (1955:266).

"Scheiss" is used in everyday German speech in quite a different manner from the way "shit" is used in Anglo-American culture. For example, if a tool broke, a man might exclaim, "Scheissding da" meaning literally "shit thing here" whereas in Anglo-American culture, one would be more likely to say, "This damn thing." Other typical expressions include "scheiss' drauf!" [shit on it] meaning roughly the equivalent of 'to hell with it' or 'what the hell?' in English. Another expression is "verdammte Scheisse" [damned shit]. Sometimes the phrase consists of intensification through doubling. "Scheissdreck" [shit-dirt] would be an example of such a doublet. A German might also say "das ist mir scheissegal" [It is to me shit same] meaning it's all the same to me, or I don't give a damn (shit) or I don't care. Another popular idiom is "Die Kacke ist am dampfen" [The shit is steaming] which means that the situation is really bad, "all hell has broken loose." One way of telling someone to mind his own business in German is: "Die Nase in den eigenen Dreck stecken" [Keep your nose in your own shit] which implies that one shouldn't put his nose in someone else's shit. In other words, take care of your own business, not somebody else's. "Der kann nicht einmal aufs Scheisshaus gehen" [He cannot go once to the shithouse] refers to someone so utterly incompetent that he can't even go to the toilet properly. There are literally dozens upon dozens of other idioms involving "Scheiss" or "Dreck" or "Arsch." These few examples are meant only to be illustrative.

I should stress that "scheiss" is not simply a common metaphor in everyday German speech habits. There is also a literal daily concern with the act of defecation. A solicitous mother may address the following rhetorical question to her infant: "Hast du die Hose voll (gemacht)?" [Have you (made) a pants full?] often accompanying the inquiry with a tender fact-finding pat on the buttocks. Similarly, a phrase of endearment in the low German dialect of Hamburg from the 1950s, frequently addressed to infants, was "Min lütten Schietbüdel" [My little shitbag] or "Min lütten Schieter" [My little shitter]. A more widespread quasi-affectionate idiom addressed to little boys is "Du kleiner Hosenscheisser" [You little pants shitter] which conveyed the connotation of 'little rascal' as far back as the sixteenth century (Spalding 1974:1374). Many adult Germans ask themselves each morning, "Werde ich heute Stuhlgang haben?" [Will I have a bowel movement today?]. Family members may typically question one another on this matter at some length. Such frank discussions often shock or surprise American listeners unfamiliar with this facet of German culture. A traditional rhyme attests to the general satisfaction felt in connection with the first act of defecation of the day: Am besten ist der Morgenschiss auch wenn er am Abend is(t). [The best thing is the morning shit even if it is in the evening.]

If the first act of defecation of the day is commonly remarked in German culture, we should not be surprised to learn that the very first act of defecation in an individual's life may also be noticed. The folk term is "der Heidendreck" [heathen or pagan shit] (Spalding 1972:1272). The expression refers to what is known in medical parlance as meconium, the dark green material in the large intestines of the full term fetus, which upon the birth of the infant becomes that infant's first feces. The reference to heathen had to do with the infant's being as yet unbaptized.

The easy acceptance of such topics in daily life in contemporary Germany is signaled by an extensive four-part serial article "Die Geschischte des Klo" [The History of the Water Closet] which appeared in Der Stern in 1979 (Vetten 1979). Stern is a popular magazine along the lines of Life and Time in the United States. It is hard to imagine Life or Time featuring a forty-page pictorial essay on the history of bathrooms complete with discussions of toilet paper and pictures of antique chamber pots. (See Figures 2-3.)

Another concrete illustration of the same tendency is a pub in Berlin called the "Klo." In order to enter this establishment frequented by middle class youth, one is obliged to put a ten pfenning piece in a slot in the front door exactly as one uses a coin to enter a pay toilet. Inside, some of the seats are toilets and there are toilet paper rolls on each table in lieu of napkins

Figure 1. A typical sign with a baby sitting on a chamber pot points the way to a public toilet. Photograph at the 1957 Oktoberfest in Munich by Dr. E.E. Waller, Jr.

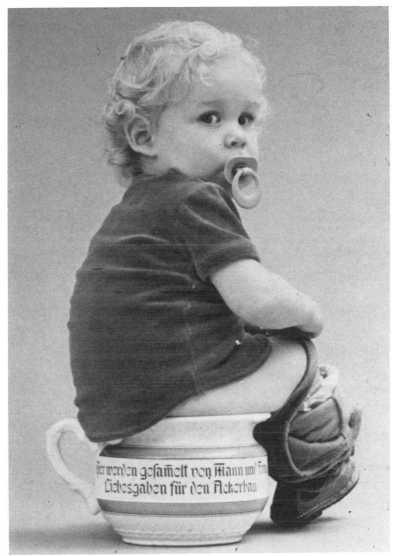

Figure 2. This and figure 3 are part of *Der Stern's* four-part serial article on the history of the water closet. It is hard to imagine *Life* or *Time* featuring a 40-page pictorial essay on the history of the bathroom. (Reprinted by permission of *Der Stern* and Black Star Photographs.)

21

Figure 3. Roll play: A German toilet-paper manufacturer clowns around. (Reprinted by permission of *Der Stern* and Black Star Photographs.)

(so that people wipe their mouths with toilet paper after eating a sandwich or drinking beer). The menu reflects the decor by offering such delicacies as "Rostbratwürstchen mit kaltem Kraut im NACHTTOPF" [Roastmeat sausage with cold cabbage in chamber pot]. (See Figures 4–6.)

The prevalence of chamber pot humor is also shown by the existence of novelty joke pots with the handle conspicuously placed on the inside of the pot. This would presumably ensure that the individual removing the pot would be forced to sully his hands with the pot's contents. One such pot, for sale in a Berlin greeting card gift shop in April 1982, contained a gauge painted on the side with the proverb "Der Mensch ist das Mass aller Dinge!" [Man is the measure of all things] with indications ranging from "kleiner Scheisser" [little shitter] at the

22

Figure 4. "The Klo," a Berlin nightclub.

bottom to "grosser Scheisser" [big shitter] close to the top. (See Figure 7.) Another chamber pot pretended to be a "Scheiss-Spiel" [shit game] involving a series of concentric circles at the bottom which encouraged the presumed user to exercise strict control over the aim and placement of his deposits.

It would be easy to multiply examples. In the same vein is a breezy compilation, *Der Furz*, assembled by Alfred Limbach (1980), which contains a generous sampling of the folklore of farting including proverbs, riddles, children's rhymes, folksongs, slang, and literary quotations on the subject. And this popular interest in matters fecal is not new. In the beginning of this century, we note that the purported memoirs of a

23

Figure 5. Inside "The Klo," some seats are toilets...

Viennese "Toilettenfrau" were published which include graffiti of the period and observations on public toilet clientele (Himmlisch 1907).

Scheisse is a theme which pervades many genres of German folklore. For example, one of the most popular pieces of contemporary German tradition consists of a series of rhymed couplets. They may be sung or recited and are sometimes found written on bathroom walls. Here is a sampling of verses, most of which I collected in Frankfurt in 1979 supplemented by additional texts from written sources (Krotus 1970:23; Rühmkorf 1972:23-24):

Scheisse in der Lampenschale	Shit in the lamp globe
gibt gedämpftes Licht im Saale.	gives dimmed light in the room.
Scheisse in den Autoreifen	Shit in the tires
gibt beim bremsen braune Streifen.	gives, when braking, brown stripes.

Figure 6. ...and there are toilet paper rolls on the tables in lieu of napkins. (Photos by B. Meiner.)

Scheisse auf dem Autodach
wird bei 100 Sachen flach.

Shit on the roof of the car
flattens out at 100 Km.

Scheisse in die Luft geschossen
gibt sehr viele Sommersprossen.

Shit shot up in the air
produces very many freckles.

The identification of freckles with feces is found elsewhere in German folklore. In 1906, a report indicates that someone who has freckles might be referred to by means of "Er hat mit dem Teufel Schissdreck gedroschen" [He has been thrashing shit with the devil] (Godelück 1906b:135).

Some of the stanzas reflect some differences of opinion on the effect of Scheisse on music:

25

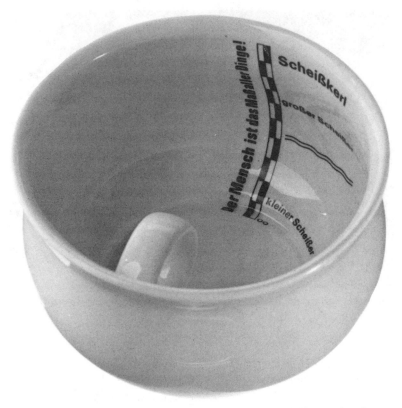

Figure 7. The prevalence of chamber pot humor is also signalled by novelty joke pots with the handle conspicuously placed on the inside of the pot. (Photo by Gene Prince).

Scheisse auf dem Grammophon verdirbt die Platte samt dem Ton.	Shit on the gramophone ruins the record including the tone.
Scheisse im Trompetenrohr bringt die schönsten Töne vor.	Shit in the trumpetbell creates the nicest sounds.
Scheisse im Trompetenrohr ersetzt den ganzen Kinderchor.	Shit in the trumpet bell replaces the whole children's choir.

Scheisse im Trompetenrohr	Shit in the trumpet bell
Kommt Gottseidank recht selten vor.	is found, thank God, very rarely.
Scheisse auf der Friedhofsmauer	Shit on the cemetery wall
stört die gäste bei der Trauer.	disturbs the guests when they are mourning.
Scheisse auf der Kirchhofsmauer	Shit on the churchyard wall
macht den frömmsten Pfarrer sauer.	makes the most pious clergyman sore.
Scheisse an des Hutes Rand	Shit on the edge of a hat
Beschmutzt beim Grüssen leicht die Hand.	easily dirties the hand when greeting.
Scheisse in der Kuchenform	Shit in the cake pan
Verändert den Geschmack enorm	changes the taste enormously,
Scheisse in den Manteltaschen	Shit in the coat pockets
verdirbt den Kindern schnell das Naschen.	quickly stops children from eating candy (on the sly).
Wenn Scheisse in der Suppe schwimmt	If shit swims in the soup
Dann sind die Gäste missgestimmt.	guests will be put in a bad mood.
Scheisse auf dem Sofakissen	Shit on the sofa cushion
Wird man wohl entfernen müssen.	probably will have to be removed.
Scheisse hinterm Sofakissen	Shit behind the sofa cushion
Lässt die Wohnkultur vermissen.	indicates a lack of gracious living.

Children's games also reflect the same scatological bias. It may be a relatively simple tonguetwister catch. One child asks another to repeat "Hirsch heiss ich" [Hirsch is my name] as fast as possible. If this phrase is rapidly repeated, the result sounds like "Hier scheiss ich" ['Here I shit'] which compels the dupe to articulate the taboo word and to "confess" the commission of the act in question. There are more elaborate games. Alfred Adler in a short essay on "Erotische Kinderspiele" briefly describes (1911:258) a variant of "Blindekuh"

[Blind Cow] which is cognate with Anglo-American Blind Man's Buff (Brewster 1953:12-16). In this game, a boy is blindfolded. Another boy urinates in his pocket or he is sprinkled by those standing around him in a circle, or the Blind Cow (the boy who is "it") is handed a piece of feces.

In a milder game called Schinkenklopfen, one child bends over, or kneels on the ground and puts his head down in the lap of another. The child in whose lap "it" has his or her head may place his hands on the side of "it's" head so that "it" cannot see behind. One member of the rest of the group comes up and hits "it" on the behind. "It" has to guess who did this. If "it" guesses correctly, the child who hit "it" becomes "it." If "it" guesses incorrectly, he must remain "it" and await further hits. Supposedly enemies will hit hard while friends will strike softly. However, sometimes clever playmates will do just the opposite so as to fool "it." In the present context, it is significant that such a children's game centers on the buttocks area of the body. This game is briefly mentioned in Jaroslav Hasek's *The Good Soldier Schwejk* (1974:85n.1) in which the game of "flesh" is described as a game among soldiers where one soldier bares his buttocks and the others hit him from behind. If he can guess which of the others has hit him, that soldier has to change places with him. The game was also included in a 1933 Nazi film entitled *Hitlerjunge Quex* and was commonly played at Nazi picnics (Bateson 1953:311).

Another game called "Stuhlraten" [chair-guessing] illustrates much the same theme. It is actually more of a trick than a game. A person claims that he can leave the room and, upon his return, identify which of three chairs someone has sat in during his absence. He leaves, after which his accomplice sits in one of the chairs. The accomplice then gets up and summons the guesser who attempts to determine which of the three chairs had been occupied. Actually, a code has previously been worked out such as the use of one word "Come" meaning the first chair, "Come in" meaning the second, and "John" (or whatever it's first name is) come in" for the third. In any event, the guesser pretends to carefully scrutinize the chairs as if to see if one of them has been moved slightly. He may put his palm or fingertips on the different seats as if to detect indentations or perhaps telltale warmth remaining from recent body contact. After considerable thought and pretended concentration, the guesser may resort to the ultimate instrument to solve the mystery: he bends down, sniffs at each of the seats in turn, and exclaims, his finger pointing triumphantly at the correct chair, "This one!"

It is more than likely that the name of the game "Stuhlraten" involves a play on "Stuhl" as both chair and (fecal) stool. Fromm, who prefers to speak of necrophilic rather than anal characters, notes that many are fascinated by bad odors. These individuals often give the impression of being "sniffers" (1973:330, 340). The emphasis upon sniffing or smelling feces is also to be found in other genres of German folklore. For example, one of the best known traditional jokes is a tale which folklorist Lutz Röhrich has meticulously traced back to the late Middle Ages in Germany (Röhrich 1967: 2:497-503). In this story, an individual discovers a beautiful flower (which obviously has a fragrant scent—it is typically a violet) or a strawberry. He covers it with his hat and rushes off to summon his wife or someone else to see it. In the meantime, a trickster comes along, removes the flower or eats the strawberry, and leaves a pile of feces under the hat. This tale, which goes back at least to the middle of the fourteenth century, is slightly reminiscent of Aarne-Thompson tale type 1528, Holding Down the Hat. It was so popular in Germany that it was frequently used as the basis for a traditional skit and not surprisingly has been reported as a Fastnachtspiel. It should be noted that playing tricks involving feces occurred in life as well as fiction. A report of a prank in the winter of 1845–46 in Schorndorf tells how the young boys who worked in a blacksmith shop smeared the hammer handles with excrement while the smiths were at supper (Bourke 1891:380-381). The popularity of such pranks would lend support to the notion (Spalding 1958:46 cf.; Reid 1967) that the possible origin of the idiom "Dreck am Stecken"—in English "to get the dirty end of the stick"— may have been occasions when someone holding a stick with excrement on one end handed it to a dupe in such a way as to befoul him. The use of the hat to display anal themes also continues to the present day. For example, in the German version of Father's Day, which takes place on the Roman Catholic feast of Ascension Thursday, all the men wear straw sailor hats adorned with toilet paper (Schalk 1971:34, 300).

Among the scatological themes which occur most often in German folklore are defecating in bed or in one's pants. Again, several examples may serve to stand for dozens of possible texts. The antiquity of the theme is affirmed by the naïve simpleton hero of Grimmelshausen's 1669 novel *Simplicius Simplicissimus* who indulges in a variety of scatological escapades. As a page at court, he asks how to pass wind quietly. He is told to raise his left leg like a dog who stands at a corner and say quietly to himself, "I fart, I fart, I fart." He tries this technique later at a formal banquet with disastrous results. Still

30

later that same evening, he tries to dance with "a lady of high nobility and great virtue." When she drew back in fear, Simplicius became panicky and screamed, "And as though that were not enough, there escaped by chance something into my trousers which emitted a most horrible smell, such as my nose had not experienced for a long time. At this moment the musicians became still, the dancers stopped and the virtuous lady on whose arm I clung thought herself highly insulted, imagining that my master had chosen to play a joke on her." Then locked in a goose-pen, Simplicius, sitting in his "own filth" observes a pair of lovers in action (1964:71-85) (much like an infant who has defecated while voyeuristically observing the primal scene of parental intercourse).

The banquet and dance sequence is reminiscent of a scene in Friedrich Dedekind's *Grobianus* of a century earlier. In *Grobianus,* a treatise on how not to behave, a youth at dinner, overcome by bladder pressure, elects to urinate in his boots. Later he is forced to dance in these boots. Then during the night, he has a stomachache, but to his dismay, he finds the doors to the outside yard locked. In desperation, he defecates into one of his boots. In the morning, not wishing to call attention to his plight, he simply puts on the boot (Rühl 1904:137-139). In another incident in this sixteenth-century satire, an individual who farts is advised to cry out, "Fie, what a stinke is this?" and if necessary put the blame on a little dog. "Say that twas he, and none but he that did the aire perfume" (1904:120, 156).

From the sixteenth century, we move to the twentieth century. There is a traditional riddle: Was ist draussen und doch drinnen? [What is outside and yet inside?] Der Dreck, wenn man sich in die Hosen beschissen hat. [Dirt when a person has shit in his pants] (Krauss and Reiskel 1905:53; cf. Polsterer, 1908:169). Ernest Borneman, in his superb collection of modern German children's folklore, specifically notes that among the three to five year olds, the counting-out rhymes tend for the most part to be scatologically oriented, concentrating upon feces and the anus (Borneman 1973:34). He includes more than forty rhymes in which dirty pants are involved (Borneman 1974:241-250). The rhymes are not new and most can be traced back for at least a century. One popular one uses the German word for "apricot" which is surely because "Aprikose" rhymes nicely with "Hose" [pants]. In this rhyme, a person typically "Frisst Aprikose, schisst in d'Hose, Gang eweck! Gang eweck. Du bist Dreck [eats apricots, shits in his pants, Go away, go away, you are filth] (Godelück 1906a:237; Ihm 1912:497; Borneman 1973:42). Sometimes, it is an adult or authority figure who is depicted in the act of defecating:

Quibus rebus cognitis
Caesar in die Hosen schiss.

In this traditional mixture of Latin and German, Caesar shits in his pants. (For versions reported in 1885, 1910, and 1960, see Ihm 1912:499; Kühlewein et al., 1910:237; and Borneman 1973:379.) This rhyme is chanted by older children, eight-to twelve-year-olds who may have had some contact with Latin. (For further discussion of Latin folk rhymes used by German schoolchildren, see Borneman 1973:379-388.)

A rhyme not requiring any knowledge of Latin is (Borneman 1974:243-244):

Karl der Grosse	Charles the Great [Charlemagne]
Hat verschissene Hose!	has shitty pants.
Karl der Kleine	Little Charles
Hat beschissene Beine.	has shitty legs.

There are also riddling questions which provide striking indices of the degree of dirtiness attained by this popular image (Krauss and Reiskel 1905:37, 53; cf. Polsterer 1980:169):

Was ist über alle Massen?	What is beyond all measure?
Wenn man in die Hosen scheisst, dass es beim Halsbande herauskommt.	When a person shits in his pants so that it comes out his collar.

or

Was ist Pech?	What is bad luck?
Wenn man in die Hosen scheisst, dass der Dreck beim Krawatl herauskommt.	When a person shits in his pants so that the dirt comes out by his tie.

In a metaphorical sense, it is perfectly reasonable for counting-out rhymes to be scatological. The ostensible object of counting-out rhymes is to *eliminate* individuals (in order to select who will be "it"). Here is a representative text collected in West Berlin in 1960 (Borneman 1973:41; cf. Rühmkorf 1967:33-34):

1,2,3,4,5,6,7,8,9	1,2,3,4,5,6,7,8,9
Wie heisst dein Kleiner Freund?	What is the name of your little friend?
Herbert!	Herbert!
Herbert hat ins Bett geschissen	Herbert has shit in bed
Gerade aufs Paradekissen!	Right on the good pillow.
Mutter hat's gesehn—	Mother has seen it
Und du kannst gehn!	And you can go (out).

33

Here we have an echo of the infant's act of defecation as a gift, an unwelcome gift for the mother. After a child messes his pants, the annoyed parent might very well say in idiomatic German, "Da haben wir die Bescherung" or "Das ist eine schöne Bescherung." Bescherung also refers to a presentation of gifts, typically at Christmas . Thus the idiom might be translated as "Here we have a fine [or pretty] mess." The idea of presenting feces as a gift is also expressed in riddle form. For example, "Was ist unverschämt?" [What is the height of impertinence?] "Jemand an seinem Geburtstage vor die Tür zu scheissen und seine Visitenkarte hineinstecken." [To shit on somebody's front door on his birthday and then put one's visiting-card on it.] The depositing of feces as a "calling card" is reminiscent of the custom of *grumus merdae* of burglars (Hellwig 1905; Reik 1949:76-81; Friedman 1968) which was practiced in Germany among other places.

But it is not just children whose folklore contains allusions to defecation in bed or in pants. The following joke collected from a German-American platoon leader in the U.S. Army in 1947 is surely representative of German adult humor:

Frederick the Great wants to show a visiting potentate how well disciplined Prussian troops are. He calls out the name of one of his men. "Private Otto Schmidt!" Schmidt snaps to attention. Frederick instructs him to stand fast until further notice. He then summons five or six of his best marksmen to form a firing squad. They load their guns—with blanks or bullets only Frederick the Great knows. He orders them to ready, aim, fire at Schmidt. They do so. Otto Schmidt does not flinch. Again, Frederick commands the firing squad to shoot. Again, Otto Schmidt does not flinch. For a third time, Frederick orders the squad to fire and for a third time, Otto Schmidt does not flinch. The visiting potentate is duly impressed with such a display of discipline. Frederick the Great then approaches Otto

Schmidt, saying, "Otto Schmidt, you have done well. You have demonstrated the bravery and courage expected of a good Prussian soldier. You may now have as a reward anything in the world you would like. What would you like?" Private Schmidt's response, "A fresh pair of pants, sir." (For a Russian-Polish version of this joke, see Blinkiewicz 1911:340.)

In a bilingual context, of course, the very name Schmidt may suggest shit. In any event, the idea of involuntary defecation as a symptom of fear is to be found in German satire through the centuries (Cf. Wittenwiler 1956:158).

The idiom "sich bekacken" [to beshit oneself] as well as "die Hosen voll haben" [to have one's pants full] according to Spalding (1974:1373, 1420) refer to defecation caused by fright. (We have in English the idiom of being scared shitless, that is, of being so frightened as to shit uncontrollably or to be unable to defecate.) There is an interesting piece of German folk speech which bears out the positive association of anal retention in a time of crisis. The idiom is "Die Arschbacken zusammenkneifen" which means literally "to tightly press or pinch the cheeks of the ass together." Metaphorically, it means to die, to stand at attention, to be brave. During World War II, the phrase was used to exhort soldiers not to be cowards. In other words, it implied that if one is afraid, one shits. Thus keep your cheeks together, be brave (and don't shit). The association of death is that one must be strong to face death and also that brave soldiers die. A modern pseudo-fable collected in Freiburg in the summer of 1979 confirms the importance of positioning one's posterior:

Eine Maus ist auf der Flucht vor einer Katze. Auf der Wiese steht eine Kuh, die gerade einen Kuhfladen macht, der glücklicherweise auf die Maus fällt. Nur die Schwanzspitze schaut noch heraus. Die

Katze zieht die Maus am Schwanz aus dem Kuhfladen heraus, reinigt sie und frisst sie auf.

Moral: 1. Nicht jeder, der dich bescheisst, meint es mit dir schlecht.

2. Nicht jeder, der dich aus der Scheisse zieht, meint es mit dir gut.

3. Wenn du schon in der Scheisse steckst, so ziehe wenigstens den Schwanz ein.

A mouse was being chased by a cat. A cow was standing in the meadow and was just dropping a cow pie which fortunately fell on the mouse. Just the tail stuck out. The cat pulled the mouse out by the tail, cleaned it off, and ate it.

The moral of this story is:

1. Not everyone who shits on you means you ill.

2. Not everyone who pulls you out of the shit means you well.

3. If you find yourself in the shit, at least pull your tail in.

It is possible that readers may feel that jokes like the preceding are to be found in many cultures and that it is unfair to cite such jokes as indicative of the inclinations of German personality. I would like to ask such readers if they can match the following exemplar of German folklore on the subject of feces. It was collected at the turn of the present century. Entitled "Der Wunsch" [The Wish], it combines the pleasure of the act of defecation with a veritable litany of aggressive impulses (Polsterer 1908:147-148).

Nichts, o Freund, kann uns heinieden Glücklich machen und zufrieden	Nothing, oh friend, in this life can make us happy and content
Liebe, Schönheit, Geld und Ehre Übermut in jeder Sphäre;	Love, beauty, money, and honor excessive merriment in all areas;

Nichts vermag uns zu erheitern,	Nothing may give us cheer
Wenn es mangelt an dem Weitern;	if the following is missing.
Fehlt nun aber dieses eine,	But if this one thing is lacking
O dann trauere und weine!	Oh then grieve and weep!
Musst du dieses eine lassen,	If you have to do without this,
Wirst du ohne Grund erblassen.	You will die needlessly.
Dieses eine, was auf Erden	This is the one thing on earth
Allen nur zum Heil kann werden,	that alone can make everyone
	healthy.
Wünsch ich dir mit frommem	I wish you in all sincerity
Munde	today at this very hour
Heut zu dieser hohen Stunde	
Dieses eine, wie soll's heissen?	This one thing, what should it be
Freund, es heisst das edle	called?
Scheissen!	Friend, it is the noble act of shitting!
Scheisse noch so viele Jahre	Go on shitting for as many years
Als auf deinem Haupte Haare,	as there are hairs on your head.
Scheiss zu allen Tagesstunden	Shit at all hours of the day
Und nach oben, sowie unten,	and upwards as well as downwards.
Scheiss am Abend, scheiss am	Shit in the evening, shit in the
Morgen,	morning
Scheiss auf alle deine Sorgen,	Shit on all your cares.
Scheiss auf Hoheit, Macht und	Shit on authority, power, and honor
Ehre,	Shit in all directions.
Scheisse über Kreuz und Quere,	
Scheiss nach Süden und nach	Shit to the south and to the north
Norden,	Shit on rank and on medals.
Scheiss auf Würden und auf Orden,	
Scheiss ins Bett und in die Hosen,	Shit in bed and in the pants
Scheiss auf Tschechen und	Shit on Czechs and Frenchmen.
Franzosen,	
Scheiss auf Schuster und auf	Shit on the shoemaker and the tailor
Schneider,	Shit on your own clothes.
Scheiss auf deine eignen Kleider,	

Scheiss auf ganze Länder, Reiche,	Shit on whole countries and
Scheiss in Seen und in Teiche,	kingdoms
	Shit in lakes and in ponds.
Scheiss in alle Strassengräben	Shit in all the roadside gutters
Scheiss sie voll und nicht daneben,	Shit them full and don't miss.
Scheiss bei Sturm, bei Wind und	Shit in storm, in wind, and weather
Wetter,	Shit on aunts and on cousins.
Scheiss auf Tanten und auf Vetter,	
Scheiss, dass alle Fenster krachen,	Shit so that all the windows crack
Scheiss überhaupt auf alle Sachen	Shit in general on everything.
Scheiss mit Kraft von zehn	Shit with the force of ten cannons
Kanonen,	so that the sun is obscured by
Dass verdunkelt wird die Sonnen,	darkness.
Scheisse fort und ohne Ende,	Shit on and without end
Scheiss dir selbst noch in die	Shit even into your own hands.
Hände,	
Scheiss sogar in dein Gesicht,	Shit even in your face
Scheisse auch auf dies Gedicht:	Shit also on this poem:
Nur auf deinen Freund scheiss	Only on your friend, don't shit!
nicht!	

Sections of this remarkable text evidently occur independently. For example, compare the final lines with the following verse reported in Vienna in 1850 (Luedecke 1907:321):

Scheiss, dass die Felsen krachen!	Shit so that the rocks crack.
Scheiss dem Teufel in seinen	Shit down the devil's throat.
Rachen!	Shit into the face of the peasant—
Scheiss dem Bauern ins Gesicht—	only not on our friendship!
nur auf unsere Freundschaft nicht!	

Another version purporting to be a name-day wish (Brenneisl 1908:272) ends as follows:

Scheisse auf Advokaten und auf Pfaffen,	Shit on lawyers and priests
Scheisse dir selber in den Rachen,	Shit yourself in the throat,
Scheisse dir selber ins Gesicht,	Shit yourself in the face,
Nur auf mich scheisse nicht!	only don't shit on me!

I would think that even the most skeptical readers might concede in the light of such textual evidence that German folklore does indicate some interest in feces and the act of defecation. But, it might be argued, so what if there are occasional scatological items of German folklore? Surely the content of folklore is vastly different from the content of formal, elitist literature. The response to that is that German so-called high culture reflects precisely the same themes. For example, one can find a number of literary texts which extol the toilet. In these paeans of praise which might be dubbed "odes to commodes," one finds consistent expressions of appreciation for the toilet and for time spent sitting on it. An early example is the "Ode an den Leibstuhl" by Alois Blumauer, written in the late eighteenth century (Blumauer 1884:6-7, reprinted in Englisch 1928b: 182-183; and Coturnix 1979:111-112), but perhaps one of the most rhapsodic testaments is by none other than Bertolt Brecht in Act I, Scene 3 of his 1918 play entitled *Baal* (Brecht 1971:13-14):

> Orge said to me:
>
> The spot on earth he most had come to crave
> Was not the grass plot by his parents' grave
>
> Or any whore's bed or confession stool
> Or snowy bosom, soft and warm and full.
>
> Orge said to me: His best retreat
> On earth had always been the toilet seat.
>
> For there a man can sit, content to know

That stars are overhead, and dung below.

A lovely place it is where even on
His wedding night a man can be alone.

A humble place where you will humbly know
You're only human, so you may as well let go.

A place of wisdom, where you clear the way
For the drink and victuals of the coming day.

A place where by exerting gentle pressure
A man can benefit while reaping pleasure.

You find out what you are in these dank pits
A man who feeds his face and meanwhile—sits.

The classic 1928 novel of World War I, Erich Maria Remarque's *Im Westen Nichts Neues* [*All Quiet on the Western Front*] contains a similar celebration of an outdoor military latrine:

> "On the right side of the meadow a large common latrine has been built, a roofed and durable construction. But that is for recruits who as yet have not learned how to make the most of whatever comes their way. We want something better. Scattered about everywhere there are separate, individual boxes for the same purpose. They are square, neat boxes with wooden sides all round, and have unimpeachably satisfactory seats. On the sides are hand grips enabling one to shift them about.
>
> We move three together in a ring and sit down comfortably. And it will be two hours before we get up again.
>
> ...Here in the open air though, the business is entirely a pleasure... We feel ourselves for the time being better off than in any palatial, white-tiled "convenience." *There* it can only be hygienic; *here* it is beautiful.
>
> These are wonderfully care-free hours. Over us is the blue sky... We read letters and newspapers and smoke...The three boxes stand in the midst of the glowing red field-poppies. We set the lid of the margarine tub on our knees and so have a good table for a game of skat...One could sit like this forever." (Remarque 1958:12-14.)

40

Rollfinke (1977:175) remarks that the passage was omitted from the first English translations of the book, presumably for the same puritanical reasons that the word "shit" was left out of English and American dictionaries for decades (cf. Mieder 1978).

There is much scatological folklore in the German military— like the military in other cultures no doubt. For example, according to one anecdote, the officers labeled their latrine with the inscription "Für die Herren Offiziere" [For the Officers] whereupon the enlisted men countered by placing an inscription on their latrine: "Für die anderen Arschlöcher" [For the other assholes] (Collofino 1939:77).

It is by no means just the military latrines in Germany which are relevant here. The construction of ordinary household toilets has been noticed by Erica Jong in her popular novel *Fear of Flying.* She protests what she calls the German's "fanatical obsession with the illusion of cleanliness. Illusion, mind you, because Germans are really not clean...just go into any German toilet and you'll find a fixture unlike any other in the world. It has a cute little porcelain platform for the shit to fall on so you can inspect it before it whirls off into the watery abyss, and there is, in fact, no water in the toilet until you flush it. As a result German toilets have the strongest shit smell of any toilets anywhere. (I say this as a seasoned world traveler)" (Jong 1974:21-22).

Even discounting the bias and vitriol in a non-German novelist's account, the fact remains that the architectonics of German toilets make it almost impossible for an individual not to see his feces after an act of defecation. It sits firmly in place on a veritable throne, ready for inspection as it were. Often the flow of water is insufficient to entirely remove the feces, and in

41

that event toilet etiquette requires one to use a toilet brush which typically stands in a small rack in the corner of the bathroom in order to properly cleanse the pedestal for the next occupant.

In a book written in 1939, one even finds a complaint registered against the newer model of toilets. From a medical standpoint, it is argued (Collofino, 1939:623), such toilets are poorly constructed inasmuch as the excrement is hidden in the depths of the toilet bowl and therefore not visible for inspection. The writer much prefers the flat bowls in which one can observe one's excretion. Alexander Kira in his architecturally oriented book *The Bathroom* claims that "the old-fashioned 'washdown' closet" is still widespread in parts of Europe, particularly Germany, and he reports, "My medical friends there assure me that the daily examination of one's feces is still considered a sound and common health practice, as it was in Pliny's time" (Kira 1976:95).

An extraordinary literary sketch of the German's concern for examining stools daily is found in Heinrich Böll's novel *Group Portrait with Lady*, published in 1971. In this novel, which led to Böll's receiving the Nobel Prize for Literature in 1972, a nun named Sister Rahel at a girls' boarding school took it upon herself to examine the "products of youthful digestion in solid and liquid form...The girls were required not to flush away these products into the invisible regions before Rahel had inspected them." And she kept records. "Taking two hundred and forty school days as an annual average, times twelve girls and five years of floor-service (as a kind of monastic duty sergeant), it is no trick to calculate that Sister Rahel kept statistical records and condensed analyses of some twenty-eight thousand eight hundred digestive processes: an astounding compendium that would probably fetch any price as a scatological and urinological document" (Böll 1973:34-35; for further discussion of anality in Böll's novel, see Rollfinke 1977:231-267).

Lest anyone mistakenly think that the above passage is but an ephemeral literary flash in the pan, he has only to read the "Inspection of Feces" section of Günter Grass's novel *The Flounder* (1978:237-241) which includes such lines as "During her years as an abbess, for instance, Fat Gret made all the novices bring her their chamber pots, and every kitchen boy who came to her for employment had first to demonstrate his fitness by showing healthy stools." Grass goes on to describe the joys in primitive times of collective group shitting: "After the horde shit-together we felt collectively relieved and chatted happily, showing one another our finished products, drawing pithy comparisons with past performances, or teasing our constipated comrades, who were still squatting in vain."

No discussion of the preoccupation of Germans with anal matters would be complete without some mention of what is probably the most popular (and insulting) invitation in all Germany: "Leck mich im Arsch." The watered-down English equivalent of "Kiss (rather than lick) my ass" does not really occupy a similar role in Anglo-American folk speech. (For parallels in other languages, see Collofino 1939:1042-1045; or Schramm 1967:145-156.) Indeed, it is difficult to convey the pervasiveness of the ass-licking metaphor in German culture. (See all the slang terms under "anilingere" in Borneman, 1971:35.18.) Whole books have been devoted to documenting the occurrences in literature and life of this one insult. Literally dozens upon dozens of proverbs, riddles, folksongs, folktales, jokes, folk poems, etc. depend upon the articulation of "Leck mich im Arsch" (henceforth LMIA) for their impact.

Indisputably the most famous literary reference to LMIA is Goethe's early play *Götz von Berlichingen* published in 1773. In this drama, based upon the life of an adventurous, individualistic knight of former times, brave Götz is finally surrounded by his enemies and about to be captured. From outside his window he hears a request that he surrender unconditionally. His famous answer: "Sag deinem Hauptmann: vor Ihro Kayserliche Majestät habe ich, wie immer, schuldigen Respekt. Er aber, sag's ihm, kann mich im Arsch lecken!" [Tell your captain that in the presence of the Imperial Majesty, I have, as always, all due respect, but as for him, tell him he can kiss my ass!] And with that Götz slams the window shut. This scene is so indelibly etched in the minds of the German intelligentsia that one need only refer to the Götz-Zitat, the Götz quote, to evoke or convey the sense of the gesture in question (Goethe, 1965:84; Schramm, 1967:16).

Thanks to the report of G. M. Gilbert, a German-speaking American intelligence officer who served as prison psychologist at the Nuremberg trial of the Nazi war criminals, we have a striking twentieth-century example of the Götz-Zitat. Gilbert attended group lunch hour conversations almost daily and visited each of the accused in his cell; immediately afterward he recorded his notes on the conversations. In one of these lunch hour conversations, Hermann Goering, who had been Reichsmarschall and Luftwaffe-Chief as well as President of the Reichstag, expressed his great annoyance at Nazi witnesses who were testifying for the prosecution against him and the other defendants. Here is Gilbert's account: "You won't see

44

me bothering to ask such a swine any questions!" Goering answered, then he turned to the audience in general and said out loud, banging his fist on the table, 'Dammit, I just wish we could all have the courage to confine our defense to three simple words: Lick my arse! Götz was the first to say it and I'll be the last!' He repeated the proposed defense with great relish, telling how Götz had said it, how another general had said it, and how he would say it" (Gilbert 1947:113).

Although Goethe's mention of LMIA is probably the best known literary allusion, it is by no means the earliest one. In Grimmelshausen's *Simplicius Simplicissimus* of 1669, one hundred years earlier than Goethe's classic account, we find a number of graphic illustrations. Six soldiers are captured by peasants. The six soldiers are directed to stand one behind the other. The peasants shoot the first five dead, but the bullet, after piercing five bodies, does not reach the sixth. The peasants cut off the sixth's nose and ears "after forcing him to lick the behinds" of five of them. The peasants then bury this surviving soldier alive.

Soon thereafter, another group of soldiers approaches. They shoot all the peasants except for five whom they take prisoner and they rescue their buried comrade. "Among the prisoners were four to whom the mutilated horseman a short while ago had had to pay his shameful homage." The soldiers debate what to do with the prisoners.

> At last one soldier stepped forward and said: "Gentlemen, as it is a shame on the whole soldiery that this villain (and he pointed to the rider) has been tortured so horribly by five peasants, so it is fair that we wipe away this blemish by making these rascals lick the horseman a hundred times"...Finally, all agreed that each of the peasants who had cleaned the rider should make it good on ten

45

soldiers and should say each time: "Herewith I wipe out the shame done to the soldiers when one of them licked our bottoms!"

When the peasants refuse to lick, they are tied over a tree-trunk "so that their buttocks were stretched upwards." They are beaten "until the red juice ran." "That is the way," the soldiers said, "in which to dry up your purified bottoms, you villains" (Grimmelshausen 1964:40-41).

This is not the only allusion to LMIA in *Simplicius*. Elsewhere, the narrator-hero triumphs over his adversary whom he catches in the act of trying to steal sheep. The antagonist is frightened. "He filled his trousers to the brim so that nobody could stand near him." The peasant owner of the sheep had this response to the robbers: "To hell with them, let them lick my behind and my sheep's behinds!" and so the defeated enemy is forced "to kiss three sheep—as many as they had intended to steal—on their bottoms." The enemy, who is encountered much later in the novel, referred to this act as "the most humiliating shame on earth" (Grimmelshausen 1964:175, 296).

It would serve little purpose to multiply literary instances of LMIA, but a few sample illustrations of LMIA folklore should suffice to indicate the nature of the tradition. (These items of folklore will probably not strike most Anglo-American audiences as particularly amusing. But that is partly the point for German audiences evidently do in some sense enjoy such folklore.) Here is a catch: "Was können Sie, ich aber nicht?" [What can you do that I cannot?] "Mich im Arsch lecken" (Krauss and Reiskel 1905:52; Polsterer 1908:169). Or "Warum hat der Hase vorn kürzere und rückwärts längere Füsse?" [Why do hares have short legs in front and longer legs in back?] "Dass

46

man ihn leichter im Arsch lecken kann." [So that one can more easily lick them in the ass] (Krauss and Reiskel 1905:41). Among the numerous jokes which center on LMIA, here is one which I collected from a German folklorist attending an international meeting in Edinburgh in August 1979: Two friends meet. One asks the other to explain to him Einstein's theory of relativity. "That's a simple matter," the other replies. He lets down his pants and demands that the questioner put his nose into his ass. "Do you see that now your nose is in my ass. We both have a nose in the ass, but I feel relatively good and you feel relatively bad." (In some versions of the joke, the dupe responds, "And this is how Einstein earned his living?")

LMIA is so popular in Germany that it has generated traditional formulas to mitigate its use and to respond to its utterance. For example, one formula pretends to be a plea for eternal friendship (Kühlewein 1909:401; Collofino 1939:842):

Leck mich am Arsch und bleib mein Freund,
Bis dir die Sonn' in's Arschloch scheint.

Lick me in the ass and remain my friend
until the sun shines in your asshole.

This, of course, involves a circumlocution for "always," analogous to the circumlocutions for "never" surveyed by Archer Taylor (1949). Among the traditional retorts to LMIA invitations is: "Ich leck keine Sau (oder Hund) am Arsch" [I don't lick pigs (or dogs) in the ass] (Gödeluck 1906:142).

One question which arises is whether or not LMIA actually occurs and if so, with what frequency. One chronicler describes a dance craze in the sixteenth century "in which male dancers were lasciviously licking the exposed behinds of their partners (Schalk 1971:329) but a traditional riddle suggests that

47

the practice of LMIA is relatively rare (Schlicktegroll 1909:9, cf. Krauss and Reiskel 1905:57):

Das erste ist der Schiffe Feind,	The first is the enemy of ships [Leck, the noun, means a leak which would be a danger to a ship].
Das zweite stets mich selber meint.	The second always means myself.
Das dritte ist Präposition,	The third is a preposition.
Das vierte schmuckt jedweden Thron.	The fourth adorns every throne [toilet seat].
Das ganze wird sehr oft begehrt	The whole is very often requested [LMIA]
Doch selten wird es nur gewährt.	Yet rarely is it ever accorded.

It is difficult to ascertain the frequency of occurrence of anal-inctus from folklore texts alone inasmuch as many of the allusions are surely meant to be taken tongue in cheek. (For a discussion of the variations in usage and nuance of the LMIA phrase, see Zintl 1980.) Ass licking, of course, implies eating shit, and it is the confusion of the oral and the anal which constitutes the ultimate degradation (Waldheim 1910:405):

Wer Scheisse frisst, der ist ein Wicht ein feiner Mann frisst Scheisse nicht.	Who eats shit is a sorry creature a well-bred man doesn't eat shit.

If the Germans do have a penchant for anal metaphors, one may ask to what extent has this tendency been noticed. Since Germans make no secret of their folklore and their literature, it is not exactly difficult to observe this undeniable facet of

German national character. Nevertheless, my impression is that the major scholarly treatises on German culture written by philosophers, political scientists, and historians make no mention whatsoever of scatological themes or preferences in Germany. However, occasional popular books have remarked on the matter (e.g., Vetten 1983). Sometimes these books are written by non-Germans or by Germans writing for non-Germans. It has even been suggested that Germans prefer anal to genital allusions. For example, in an introduction to a 1972 English translation of *A Pleasant Vintage of Till Eulenspiegel,* an edition of Till Eulenspiegel's merry pranks dating from 1515, Paul Oppenheimer comments "that while Eulenspiegel ignores sex and love, he delights in shit. In a great many of his adventures he uses either his own or other people's excrement as a weapon, an instrument of revenge, or a device for embarrassment. In Chapter 24, he wins the title of champion buffoon from the King of Poland by eating his own excrement with a spoon; in Chapter 91, he humiliates a devious priest by forcing him to drench his hands in excrement camouflaged with coins ... But the point here is that ... Eulenspiegel seems to enjoy human excrement to the exclusion of sex and love" (1972:xx-xxi). For woodcuts showing Till Eulenspiegel in the act of defecating, see figure 8. See also Collofino 1939:988-989; for the theory that the name Till Eulenspiegel derives from expressions meaning "Leck mich im Arsch," see Collofino 1939:1048. First proposed by Ernst Jeep near the end of the nineteenth century, the controversial theory suggests that the original initial portion of the character's name derives from "ulen" meaning to wipe or clean and that "spiegel" refers to the posterior portion of the anatomy (Jeep 1896:273-275). This proposed meaning of 'wipe-ass' is confirmed by modern German folk

Figure 8. "Eulenspiegel seems to enjoy human excrement to the exclusion of sex and love." (Courtesy of the Department of Rare Books and Special Collections, Firestone Library, Princeton University.)

speech (Borneman 1971) and would certainly be appropriate in the light of the frequency of anal adventures in the Eulenspiegel cycle. We find a similar sentiment expressed in the translator's commentary on Wittenwiler's fifteenth-century peasant satire of epic life, *The Ring:* "Whereas all excretory functions are discussed openly, reproductive organs and functions are usually described by displacements and circumlocutions" (Wittenwiler 1956:155).

We can trace this same preference to the twentieth century. Austrian-Jewish writer Jakov Lind during World War II disguised himself as a Dutchman and brazenly hid out in Germany itself by working on canal barges. On one boat, the skipper was an old man in his seventies named Bacher. In his autobiography, *Counting My Steps,* Lind offers the following details of his life in 1944:

"Bacher, whose hands were constantly trembling, was a loud-mouthed, angry old man, who wouldn't let a sentence pass without the word Scheisse, in spite of the fact that his wife reminded him with a reproachful 'But, Eduard, is that necessary?'" Lind sometimes worked too slowly which prompted such abuse as:

"Lift your feet you Scheisskerl, you Scheiss-holländer, a little quicker you Arschloch, you Holländischer Schweinehund." (Little did he know that I was a Saujude as well. Had he known that, he would have pushed me overboard with his own hands, knowing that I couldn't swim.) Our quarrels never ended. And as the war went better for us, I got more self-confident and once let myself go to say the most humiliating thing one can ever say to a German: 'Leck mich am Arsch,' meaning "lick my arse." Unlike the rest of the world, the Germans have no use for the expressive term "fucking." The word "fucking" can only be used when it means just that. What is considered dirty and therefore insulting by the Anglo-Saxons means nothing to the Germans. For them, everything that has to do with the rear end, faeces, and the anus is real filth. That's why the words Arsch, Scheisse, Arschloch, and "Lick my arse" are real and serious insults." (Lind 1969:126-127).

In similar fashion, George Bailey in his book *Germans* states, "It is often pointed out that German profanity relies heavily on the fecal—Klugscheisser ('smart-shitter') for 'wise guy'; a situation is 'beschissen' ('shat-upon')—and the scatological to the almost total exclusion of the sexual" (Bailey 1972:128).

51

Adolph Schalk, American son of an Austrian-born immigrant mother, in his book on the Germans published in 1971 offers the following comment:

> Shocking to many Americans is the Germans' earthiness about natural processes. Instead of the discreet "lavatory" or "powder room" the Germans use the straightforward Toilette or W.C. (literally, Wasser Closet and irreverently used in reference to Winston Churchill during World War II). Instead of showing pictures of their nude babies lying prostrate as Americans are wont to do, beaming German parents think it is hilariously funny to display snapshots of their toddlers sitting on the pot. (Schalk 1971:51).

There is ample evidence in German folklore to support the notion that genital matters are commonly expressed in terms of anal equivalents. For example, consider the following aphoristic complaint.

> Alte Jungfern sagen von den Männern:
> Old maids say about men:
>
> Sie sind wie Eisenbahn-Klos:
> They are like railroad train toilets:
>
> Entweder besetzt oder beschissen.
> Either occupied or shitty.

Here is a typical joke in southern German dialect which explicitly plays upon the possibility of substituting anal for genital activity (Anon. 1968:172):

> "Guat geschissn ist halbat gvöglt" — auch ein schöner Stuhlgang hat sein Angenehmes — , sagt der Knecht zum Bauern. Der Bauer: "Scheiss halt nohmal, na hast gvöglt und lasst meini Menscher in Ruah!"
>
> "A good shit is like half a fuck" — also a beautiful bowel movement has its pleasant aspects, said the hired hand to the farmer. The

farmer: "Then go shit again and you will have a full fuck and leave my wenches alone."

But it is not the equivalence of anal and genital acts which is of interest in the present context. Rather it is the favoring of the anal over the genital, an esthetic judgment made once again by the Germans themselves in their folklore. Consider the following revealing couplet (Waldheim, 1910:404):

Gut Scheissen das kann sehr beglücken	Good shitting, that can make one very happy
vielmehr noch als manchmal das Ficken.	much more even than sometimes fucking.

This unequivocal articulation once again demonstrates how folklore expresses in a direct and uncensored fashion important native views of the world. In this case, such folklore shows that the idea that Germans might rank anal pleasure on a par with or even superior to genital pleasure is not just some idle speculation on the part of an armchair observer from outside the culture. An interesting folksong collected in Westphalia before World War I provides a dramatic confirmation of this tendency (Schnabel 1970:39-40):

Des Mädchens Klage	The Maiden's Complaint
Es sitzt bei fahlem Mondenschein	She sits in the pale moonlight
Allein in ihrer Kammer	alone in her room
Die schönste Jungfrau, tugendrein	the most beautiful virgin, chaste
Und ringt die Händ voll Jammer.	and wrings her hands in despair.
Ach, Gott, schluchzt sie, ach; wär ich tot,	Oh God, she sobs, oh, if I were dead
Ich wollte mich nicht grämen;	I wouldn't be so sad;
Doch was mir heut tat ein Fallot	What a scoundrel did to me today
Darob muss ich mich schämen.	I have to be terribly ashamed of.

Da kommt der Kerl zu mir herein,	There came this fellow in here to me
Die Tür war nicht verschlossen;	The door was not locked;
Ich hätte können zwar mal schrein	To be sure I could have just
Doch hats mich grad verdrossen.	screamed,
Er küsste mich gar glühend heiss,	But I was really annoyed.
und kroch zu mir ins Bettchen,	He kissed me very passionately
Er gab mir süsse Namen, leis,'	and crept in bed with me.
Spielt er mir an dem Gröttchen.	He whispered sweet names to me;
	He played with my "little grotto,"
Ich armes Ding, ich dulde still —	Poor me, I suffered it quietly —
Und leg mich in Parade:	and put myself on display.
und denk, ich tue, was er will,	and I'm thinking I'll do what he
	wants.
Schon ist sein Schwanz gerade.	Already his penis is erect.
Da plötzlich steht er auf im Bett,	Then all of a sudden he gets up in
Mein Loch fängt an zu beissen,	bed,
Ich halt es hin, so wonnig nett,	My hole begins to be hot
Doch ei, er tut — drauf scheissen.	I'm offering it so delightful, dainty
	But oh, he — shits on it.

Sometimes the issue is not so much a matter of anal over genital, but rather a combination of anal with genital. The buttocks is the prominent area of the body in German art and thought. From the focus of corporal punishment (as in spanking a child) to full-fledged flagellation, we find endless numbers of pictures of posteriors. The evidence for this assertion ranges from German postcards and modern advertisements (Rollfinke 1977:15, 19) to cartoons and collections of "erotic" photographs. One need only browse in Ernst Schertel's four volume *Der Flagellantismus als litarisches Motiv* (1929-1932); Alfred Kind's *Die kallipygischen Reize* (1950) or *Dir gehört der Arsch versohlt: Die erotische Freude am Popklatschen* (1979), the latter consisting essentially of a series of turn-of-the-century photographs of naked buttocks being spanked or switched, to find ample demonstration of this predilection. The game of "Schinkenklopfen," literally 'ham-beating,' described earlier is part of this same pattern.

It is in this light that one can appreciate a letter written by the celebrated 18th century aphorist Georg Christoph Lichtenberg (1742-1799) extolling the virtues of the buttocks. In this letter addressed to Georg Heinrich Hollenberg dated September 23, 1788, Lichtenberg includes a delightful message to a godchild which consists almost entirely of a list of the principal uses of the buttocks. It offers a place to be spanked when naughty, a good thing to land on when falling, and cushions essential for sitting down comfortably. In addition, Lichtenberg adds a fourth function: if some nasty fellow is reviling you and does not even have the guts to stand up to you until you've been able to box his ears, open your coat in the rear and show him your cushions. (Lichtenberg, 1959: 181-182).

The German delight in defecation is so great as to have resulted in public performances or pantomimes of the act. Famed artist and political cartoonist George Grosz participated in an evening of protest in a Berlin gallery in February of 1918. Supposedly Grosz performed "an obscene tap-dance in which he relieved himself in pantomime before a Lovis Corinth painting—"Kunst ist Scheisse!" ("Art is shit!") (Lewis 1971:57). An account of German nightlife during World War II (Bailey 1972:128) remarked that the "stripteasers and assorted exotic dancing girls . . . often confuse sex with obscenity, the erotic with the fecal, going through motions that are suggestive not of copulation but of defecation." In 1969, a young man on the stage of a University of Vienna auditorium stripped off his clothes. Then he urinated, drank the urine from his cupped hand, and vomited. For his finale, he turned his back to the audience and defecated. "He then smeared the excrement on his nude body while singing a rousing rendition of the Austrian national anthem" (Rollfinke 1977:8, citing Jurreit 1969). Even in the most avant-garde theaters in the United States, it is hard to imagine such acts occurring. And it should be stressed that this last example is by no means unique. It was evidently part of a whole "movement" called "aktionismus" in which artists or actors indulged in various "Ekel-Orgie" [Disgusting orgies], many of which were faithfully recorded for posterity on film. An extraordinary catalog, which includes the most explicit photographs imaginable of acts of defecation, smearing feces on self or others, and LMIA, as well as a list of the numerous art films made from these "happenings," documents this tradition in graphic detail (cf. Weibel 1970:43, 85-86, 129, 177, 200). One is reminded of Montaigne's comment made near the end of his *Essays* (1927:2:559) "Every nation has many habits and customs which to any other nation are not only strange but amazing and barbarous."

If one grants the abundance of fecal metaphors in contemporary German culture, the question arises as to just how far back this preoccupation can be traced. Is the German interest in Scheisse a longstanding one? In an essay claiming to discuss the two oldest pieces of scatology in German literature, Leonhardt (1911) mentions a legend of the tenth century referring to farting and also a twelfth century epic, "Salomon und Morolf," which contains extended passages of verbal dueling involving explicit excremental references. (For further discussion of Solomon and Morolf, see Collofino, 1939:837-841.) That would suggest that the pattern is at least a thousand years old.

In Tacitus' *Germania*, written in 98 A.D., we learn that the peoples of Germany have the "habit of hollowing out underground caves, which they cover with masses of manure" (Tacitus 1970:115). This shelter served as both a refuge from winter and as a storehouse for produce. But it also functioned as a sanctuary if an invader threatened because such hidden excavations either were not known to exist or were undetectable without a search. The idea of using dung as a form of defense found more elaborate expression in the custom of building fortifications. In Grimmelshausen's 1669 novel, we find allusions in piling up manure as a method of fortification (Grimmelshausen 1964:14, 49).

One might argue that the protective power of dung is also reflected in medical practices. It was commonly used in a variety of cures. The center of the so-called Dreck-Apotheke was, of course, Germany. A key work was Franz Christian Paullini's *Heilsame Dreck-Apotheke* published in Frankfurt in 1696. It was Paullini who observed (Englisch 1928:10-11) that "Dreckfresser sind wir alle" [Shiteaters are we all] insofar as most foods and fruits are fertilized with manure and many of the creatures that we eat (fish, chickens, etc.) have eaten feces. The belief in the efficacy of the "filth-pharmacy," which included internal as well as external treatments, has prevailed for many centuries. A report on traditional medicine published in 1877, for example, includes mention of "Goldsalbe" [Gold-salve] which consisted of fresh human feces placed on abscesses, especially on the sick breasts of a woman in childbed. A note explicitly states this was very widely practiced (Schüz, 1877:273). The point is that fortifying one's dwelling or one's body both made use of feces. (For a sampling of some of folk medical practices utilizing feces, see the entry under "Kot" in Hoffman-Krayer and Bächtold-Stäubli's *Handwörterbuch des deutschen Aberglaubens.*)

57

Scientific as well as folk medicine in Germany reflects the pattern. For example, in the eighteenth century, a strange theory was propounded in Germany by a physician named Johann Kämpf. According to Kämpf's "doctrine of the infarctus," the principal cause of most human ills was fecal impaction. The cure depended upon the then fashionable vogue of clysters and enemas (Friedenwald and Morrison 1940:244). German contributions in this area range from G. Friedrich Hildebrandt's three-volume *Geschichte der Unreinigkeiten im Magen und den Gedärmen [History of Impurities in the Stomach and Intestines]* (1790) to experimenting with suppositories containing such substances as cocoa butter, glycerin, and olive oil (Diepgen 1953:26). A survey devoted to the history of the enema claims "The first use of the roentgenologically opaque enema was in Germany" (Montague 1934:458). It is also of passing interest, although it may be only a coincidence, that so many of the treatises written on enemas, purgatives, suppositories, and the like are written in German (cf. Diepgen 1953; Kahl and Ehler 1970; Schertel 1976; and Zglinicki 1972).

But there is far better evidence of the longstanding German concern for Scheisse than occasional reports of fortifications made of manure or curious details in the history of medicine. One need only examine the lives and writings of some of the great minds of the German-speaking world over the centuries. If there is such a thing as German national character, one would logically expect the leading figures in the development of German culture to embody such character. We may speak of national character blithely enough, but in the final analysis, the true test of the validity of the concept comes down to

58

individual case histories. For this reason, I should like to consider briefly several individuals among the many who have achieved distinction from the German-speaking world.

Martin Luther (1483-1546) provides a rather striking example from the early sixteenth century. It was surely no accident that his critical inspiration for the idea that individual faith was more important than papal dogma, an idea which led to the Protestant Reformation, came to him from the Holy Spirit precisely while he was sitting on the privy in a tower. This "revelation in the tower" episode, as well as Luther's frequent recourse to scathing scatological metaphors, have long proved sources of embarrassment to conservative theologians. Luther's marked anality has been amply documented and discussed by Erik H. Erikson in *Young Man Luther* and by Norman O. Brown in *Life Against Death*. (For a comparison of the two analyses, see Domhoff, 1970.) Certainly, Luther's many encounters with the devil had an unmistakable anal cast. The devil's face was an anus and the devil reportedly showed Luther his posterior or farted on him. Norman Brown comments: "As passages too numerous to cite show, Luther's most general word for the assaults of the Devil is the homely German verb *bescheissen*" (1959:208). Luther fought fire with fire and his responses to the devil included the inevitable LMIA. He also told the devil "to defecate in his pants and hang them round his neck." In addition, he threatened to defecate in the devil's face or to throw the devil into his (Luther's) anus where he belonged (Brown 1959:208). With respect to the depiction of the anus as a face, it should be mentioned that this metaphor has continued in German folklore. Typically, the anus is referred to as a noseless face, e.g., "Leck mich, wo ich keine Nase habe" [Lick me where I have no nose] (Godelück 1906b:142). Luther's *Table Talk* contains numerous anal allusions, e.g., "I am like ripe shit, and the world is a gigantic ass-hole. We probably will let go of each other soon" (Erikson 1958:206; for a general discussion of Luther's conception of the devil, see Klingner 1912:18-47). There can be no question but that Luther took true pleasure in such earthy idioms and in a collection of 489 proverbs which he himself made circa 1530, he included several dozen which specifically mentioned anal activities. For example, he recorded a striking metaphor suggesting the ultimate in useless effort "Todten scheissen tragen" [Who's going to take the dead to the night pot?] (Thiele 1900:253). Dragging a corpse to position it on a chamber pot would certainly qualify as a futile and foolish waste of time.

Luther's propensity to employ anal imagery led him to describe the Pope and other members of the Catholic Church establishment in scatological terms, and this was well known in his own day. As a matter of fact, critics of Luther were sometimes inspired to reply in kind. For example, Sir Thomas More (1478–1535), canonized as a saint of the Roman Catholic Church only as recently as 1935, is presumably best known for his *Utopia* (1516) and for his adamant refusal to countenance Henry VIII's plans to divorce his queen, but among More's lesser known works is his acerbic *Responsio ad Lutherum* in 1523 intended as a reply to Luther's attack one year earlier on Henry VIII, the *Contra Henricum regem angliae*. Included in More's Responsio one finds such passages as: "for as long as your reverend paternity will be determined to tell these shameless lies, others will be permitted, on behalf of his English majesty, to throw back into your paternity's shitty mouth, truly the shit-pool of all shit, all the muck and shit which your damnable rottenness has vomited up, and to empty out all the sewers and privies onto your crown divested of the dignity of the priestly crown, against which no less than the kingly crown you have determined to play the buffoon." This diatribe is followed by a mock apology to the reader: "In your sense of fairness, honest reader, you will forgive me that the utterly filthy words of this scoundrel have forced me to answer such things for which I should have begged your leave. Now I consider truer than truth that saying: 'He who touches pitch will be wholly defiled by it.' For I am ashamed even of this necessity, that while I clean out the fellow's shit-filled mouth I see my own fingers covered with shit" (More 1969:311-313).

One is tempted to observe that even in the sixteenth century, the English were more likely to apologize for using scatological imagery than were the Germans. I am not aware that Luther ever apologized for casting his criticisms of the church in earthy anal terms.

Although Luther's scatological bias is well known, it has not been perceived in the context of German national character. Erikson is interested in Luther as an illustration of the identity crisis of the adolescent while Brown uses Luther as one of a number of examples of what he terms the excremental vision which allegedly underlies western civilization with special relevance to capitalism and Protestantism. Neither Erikson nor Brown make any inferences about Luther's being German. Gaston Vorberg, a doctor who briefly reviewed Luther's scatological expressions suggested (1926) that despite the general tendency in that era to indulge in such metaphors, Luther's repeated attacks involving anality were excessive and that they reflected a peculiarity of his personality. Without intending to take anything away from Luther's genius, I would argue that Luther was acting in accordance with general behavior patterns common then—and now—in German national character.

If Luther can be appropriately understood to be in some sense representative of the sixteenth century in Germany with respect to indulgence in scatological tendencies, can we find an exemplar of the same tradition in the seventeenth century? Fortunately, a most fascinating woman, Elisabeth Charlotte of the Palatinate (1652-1722) has left an invaluable record in her correspondence. Known affectionately as Liselotte, she married the brother of Louis XIV and lived most of her life in France. Nevertheless, she clung tenaciously to her German identity and carried out a voluminous correspondence with German friends and family. Although she counts as royalty, her letters reveal a host of earthy references to various bodily functions. One written at Fontainebleau to her aunt, the wife of the Elector of Hanover, dated October 9, 1694 (Coturnix 1979:126-127; cf. *Bibliotheca Scatologica* 1970:19-20), may serve to illustrate her inimitable style of discourse. The letter has been omitted from many of the standard editions of Liselotte's letters.

> Sie sind in der glücklichen Lage, scheissen gehn zu können, wann Sie wollen, scheissen Sie also nach Belieben. Wir hier sind nicht in derselben Lage, hier bin ich verpflichtet, meinen Kackhaufen bis zum Abend aufzuheben; es gibt nämlich keinen Leibstuhl in den Häusern an der Waldseite. Ich habe das Pech, eines davon zu bewohnen und darum den Kummer, hinausgehen zu müssen, wenn ich scheissen will, das ärgert mich, weil ich bequem scheissen möchte, und ich scheisse nicht bequem, wenn sich mein Arsch nicht hinsetzen kann. Dazu wäre noch zu bemerken, dass uns jeder beim Scheissen sieht: Da laufen Männer, Frauen, Mädchen und Jungen vorbei, Pfarrer und Schweizergarden können einander zusehen; nun, kein Vergnügen ohne Mühe und wenn man überhaupt nicht scheissen müsste, dann

fühlte ich mich in Fontainebleau wie der Fisch im Wasser. Es ist äusserst betrüblich, dass meine Freuden von Scheisshaufen behindert werden; ich wünschte, dass der, der das Scheissen erfunden hat, er und seine ganze Sippschaft, nur durch eine Tracht Prügel scheissen könnte! Wie war das am Dienstag? Man müsste leben können, ohne zu scheissen. Setzen Sie sich zu Tisch mit der besten Gesellschaft der Welt, wenn Sie scheissen müssen, müssen Sie scheissen gehen oder verrecken. Ach, die verdammte Scheisserei! Ich weiss nichts Ekiligeres als das Scheissen. Sie sehen eine hübsche Person, niedlich, reinlich, Sie rufen aus: ach wie reizend wäre das, wenn sie nicht schisse! Den Lastenträgern, Gardesoldaten, Sänftenträgern, dem Volk dieses Kalibers billige ich es zu. Aber: die Kaiser scheissen, die Kaiserinnen scheissen, die Könige scheissen, die Königinnen scheissen, der Papst scheisst, die Kardinäle scheissen, die Fürsten scheissen und die Erzbischöfe und Bischöfe scheissen, die Pfarrer und die Vicare scheissen. Geben Sie zu, die Welt ist voll von ekelhaften Leuten! Denn schliesslich scheisst man in der Luft, man scheisst auf die Erde, man scheisst ins Meer, das Weltall ist angefüllt mit Scheissern und die Strassen von Fontainebleau mit Scheisse, vor allem mit Schweizerscheisse und die pflanzen Haufen—ebensogrosse wie Sie, Madame. Wenn Sie glauben, einen hübschen kleinen Mund zu küssen, mit ganz weissen Zähnen—Sie küssen eine Scheissemühle: alle Köstlichkeiten, die Biscuits, die Pasteten, Torten, Füllungen, Schinken, Rebhühner und Fasanen usw. das Ganze existiert nur um daraus gemahlene Scheisse zu machen...

You are fortunate to be able to shit when you wish. Shit then to your heart's content. We are not in the same situation here where I am obliged to keep my shitload until evening. There is no toiletchair in the houses fronting on the woods and I have the misfortune to live in one of them and that causes the grief of having to go outside when I wish to shit and this makes me angry because I like to shit in comfort and I can't shit comfortably if my ass doesn't sit on anything. Also everyone can see you shitting: men, women, girls, boys run by; clergymen and Swiss guards can watch one another; well, there is no enjoyment without difficulty and if a person didn't have to shit at all then I would feel at Fontainebleau like a fish in water.

It is extremely depressing that my pleasures are impeded by piles of shit. I wish that he who invented shitting, I wish that he and all his kin would be able to shit only by having it beaten out of them.

How was it on Tuesday? Oh that one should be able to live without shitting? Sit down at table with the best society in the world; if you must shit, then you must go shit or die. Ah, the damned shit. I know nothing more disgusting than shitting. You see a beautiful person, neat, clean, you cry out, "how charming it would be if she didn't shit!"

I can excuse porters, guards, sedan-chair carriers, people of that low caliber, but emperors shit, empresses shit, kings shit, queens shit, the pope shits, cardinals shit, princes shit, and archbishops and bishops shit, priests and vicars shit. You have to admit the world is full of disgusting people. Because finally, people shit in the air, people shit on the earth; people shit in the sea, the universe is filled with shitters, and the streets of Fontainebleau are full of shit, above all Swiss shit and they plant piles— just as big as you, Madame. If you think you are kissing a pretty little mouth with all white teeth—you are kissing a shitmill: Every single delicacy, biscuits, pastries, tarts, fillings, hams, partridges, pheasants, etc. all of it exists only to be made into ground up shit.

This extraordinary letter contains numerous popular anal erotic themes: e.g., the idea that food is transformed into feces, the reminder that even exalted personnages are obliged to defecate. Even the allusion to a "fish in water" calls to mind the folk couplet "So, wie der Fisch im Wasser lebt, die Scheisse in dem Arschloch klebt" [As the fish lives in water, so does the shit stick to the asshole] (Waldheim 1910:405). The complaint about being observed in the act of defecation expressed in the first part of the letter is also the subject of a number of German jokes. For example, Heinrich Bebel (1472–1518), a Tübingen professor, assembled a famous collection of facetiae. Some were borrowed from literary sources, but others were collected from his Swabian surroundings. In a typical text, a noble horseman caught sight of a peasant woman who was shitting behind a tree in a field. Thinking that perhaps she might be embarrassed, he called out to her, "Well, dear girl, go on with your work for it is a thing which no one can dispense with." Thereupon the woman who had now emptied her body answered, "I can well dispense of this thing. If it pleases you, take it along with you. I will gladly make you a present of it." In another short text, a parson from Malmsheim in the village, who saw a shitting peasant, called out to him, "What are you shitting there?" Replied the peasant, "What business is it of yours? Is it no longer possible for anyone to shit without your putting your nose in it?" (Bebel 1907:112).

The eighteenth century was not without an illustrious representative. While Luther's scatological bent was and is fairly well known, Mozart's until recently was presumably known only to specialists in his biography. Yet in his letters to his family, the composer reveals a truly extraordinary fascination with anality. Indeed, I believe his indulgence in fecal imagery may be virtually unmatched. In reading Mozart's letters, one should keep in mind that he was surely trying to be funny. The point here is precisely that he, like Germans and Austrians to this day, found great humor in anal allusions. Some of the most blatant and unabashed anality in Mozart's letters is to be found in postscripts, which when one stops to think about it makes sense. References to the anus might very appropriately come at the *ends* of letters. In a letter to his sister dated March 3, 1770—Mozart, then 14, writes: P.A. Kiss Mamma's hands for me 1000000000000 times. Greetings to all our good friends and a thousand greetings to you from Catch-me-quick-and-then-you-have-me and from Don Cacarello, especially from behind." On May 2, 1770, Mozart added a postscript to a letter his father had written to his mother: "Praise and thanks be to God. I am well and kiss Mamma's hand and my sister's face, nose, mouth, neck and my bad pen and arse, if it is clean" (Anderson 1938 1:173, 197).

The practice of ending a letter with a scatological turn of phrase was evidently not peculiar to Mozart. His mother, for example, often ended her letters in similar fashion. In a letter written in 1777 to her husband Leopold Mozart, she closes, "Addio, ben mio. Keep well, my love. Into your mouth your arse you'll shove. I wish you goodnight, my dear, but first shit in your bed and make it burst. It is long after one o'clock already. Now you can go on rhyming yourself" (Anderson 1938 1:404). The ryhme, of course, is completely lost in the English translation. In German: "adio ben mio leb gesund, Reck den arsch zum mund. Ich winsch ein guete nacht, scheiss ins beth das Kracht.. " (Bauer and Deutsch 1962:14). A careful reading of Mozart's letters reveals the presence of genuine oral formulas or perhaps only written ones. For example, in one of the remarkable series of letters Mozart wrote to his cousin Maria Anna Thekla Mozart, known as the "Bäsle," dated November 5, 1777, we find: "Well, I wish you good night, but first shit into your bed and make it burst. Sleep soundly, my love, into your mouth your arse you'll shove." The German idioms are nearly the same as those employed by his mother: "lezt wünsch ich eine gute nacht, scheissen sie ins bett dass es kracht; schlafens gesund, reckens den arsch zum mund" (Bauer and Deutsch, 1962:104).

In this same letter to his cousin, Mozart comments: "ach Mein *arsch* brennt mich wie feuer! was muss das nicht bedeuten!—vielleicht will *dreck* heraus? ja ja, *dreck,* ich kenne dich, sehe dich, und schmecke dich. [My ass burns like fire. What could it mean? Perhaps some filth wants to come out, yes, yes filth, I know you, see you, taste you.] This letter to his cousin ends in the following way: "As I was doing my best to write this letter, I heard something on the street. I stopped writing—I got up—went to the window...and...the sound ceased. I sat down again, started off again to write—but I had hardly written ten words when again I heard something. I got up again—as I did, I again heard a sound, this time quite faint—but I seemed to smell something slightly burnt—and wherever I went, it smelt. When I looked out of the window, the smell disappeared. When I looked back into the room, I again noticed it. In the end, Mamma said to me: "I bet that you have let off one." "I don't think so, Mamma," I replied. "Well, I am certain that you have," she insisted. Well, I thought "Let's see," put my finger to my arse and then to my nose and—Ecce, provatum est. Mamma was right after all" (Bauer and Deutsch 1962:105; Anderson 1938 2:526–527).

The other letters Mozart wrote to his cousin constitute variations on the same theme. In one dated November 13, 1777, we find the following passage: "Verzeihen sie mir meine schlechte schrift, die feder ist schon alt, ich scheisse schon wircklich bald 22 jahr aus den nemlichen loch, und ist doch nicht verissen!—und hab schon so ofte geschissen—und mit den Zähnen den dreck ab-bissen." [Forgive my poor writing but the quill is already old; I've been shitting nearly 22 years out of the same hole and it is not yet worn out and I have already so often shat and bitten off the filth with my teeth.] (Bauer and Deutsch 1962:122; Anderson 1938 2:546). Noteworthy incidentally is Mozart's veritable equation of writing-with-ink and defecation, an equation found cross-culturally in latrinalia verse!

Mozart's letter of December 3, 1777, begins, "My very dear cousin, Before I write to you, I must go to the closet. Well, that's over. Ah! At last I feel lighter, a weight is off my heart; and now I can guzzle again." In this same letter, we find phrases such as "Huzza, copper-smith, come, be a man, catch if you can, lick my arse, copper-smith" or "If I have diarrhoea I run: and if I can't contain myself any longer, I shit into my trousers." The letter closes with "Please give a whole arseful of greetings from us both to all our good friends. . .Well, I've no more news to give you, save that an old cow has shit some new manure" and the letter is signed "W.A. Mozart, who shits without a fart" (Anderson, 1938 2:594–596). The letter dated December 23, 1778, has as postscript: "Dhit-Dibitari, the parson at Rodampl, licked his cook's arse, to show others as an example," but it is perhaps his letter of February 28, 1778, which contains one of the most passionate passages of all.

"So schreiben sie mir baldt, damit ich den brief erhalt, sonst wenn ich etwa schon bin weck, bekomme ich statt einen brief einen dreck. dreck!—dreck!—o dreck! o süsses wort!—dreck!—schmeck! auch schön!—dreck, schmeck!—dreck!—leck—o charmante!—dreck, leck! das freüet mich!—dreck, schmeck und leck!—schmeck dreck, und leck dreck!" [Write soon so that I will have a letter otherwise when I am awake, I will receive instead of a letter some "dreck." Dreck, dreck, o dreck. Oh sweet word! Dreck. Tastes good. Also beautiful. Dreck, tastes good; dreck, lick, oh, charming. Dreck, lick, that's what I like. Dreck, tastes good and lick!—

taste dreck and lick dreck] (Bauer and Deutsch 1962:308; Anderson, 1938 2:741).

Mozart's letters to his cousin, the Bäsle letters, were at one time owned by Stefan Zweig who, realizing their extraordinary nature, actually wrote to Sigmund Freud in 1931, suggesting that the letters might provide the basis for an interesting study for one of his students, but unfortunately Zweig's proposal was not followed up (Hildesheimer 1977:117–118). The present discussion does not pretend to be a full-fledged examination of Mozart's personality, but is rather intended to be merely one instance of what I take to be general German (and Austrian) national character. Mozart's letters are so full of data relevant to the present discussion that it is difficult to choose which examples to cite. A poem Mozart wrote to his mother on January 31, 1778, includes the following:

Madame Mutter!	Madame mother
Ich esse gerne Butter	I like butter.
...	...
Ich bin bei Leuten auch	I'm also with people
die tragen den Dreck im Bauch,	who carry filth in their guts
doch lassen sie ihn auch hinaus	who also let it out
So wohl vor, als nach dem Schmaus.	both before and after meals.
Gefurzt wird allzeit auf die Nacht	Farting goes on all through the night
Und immer so, dass es brav kracht.	And always so there is a crackling barrage.
Doch gestern war der fürze König	Yesterday came the king of farts
dessen Fürze riechen wie Hönig,	whose farts smelled like honey.
Wir sind ietzt über 8 Tage weck	We've been away for over 8 days
Und haben schon geschissen vielen Dreck.	And have already shit much filth.

Und das Concert spar ich mir nach Paris,	And the concerto I'll save for Paris,
Dort schmier ichs her gleich auf den ersten Schiss	There I'll scribble it down, at the first shit.
Wir beleidigen doch nicht Gott mit unserem Scheissen	We don't offend God with our shitting
Auch noch weniger, wenn wir in dreck nein beissen.	And even less, if we bite into the filth.

And this touching letter-poem to his mother ends with:

| Sie zu embrassiren und dero Händ zu küssen | (On Monday I will have the honor) of embracing you and kissing your hand |
| Doch werd' ich schon vorhero haben in die Hosen geschissen. | But before that I will already have shit in my pants. |

The letter is signed Trazom, which is Mozart spelled backward (Bauer and Deutsch 1962:245–247; Anderson 1938 2:673–675).

Ernest Jones in his delineation of anal erotic character traits called special attention to the tendency to be occupied with the reverse side of various things and situations. One instance of this, according to Jones, is reversing words and letters in writing (Jones 1961:423; cf. Abraham 1953:390). Mozart frequently reversed words and letters—as did his father Leopold (Anderson 1938 2:519; for examples of Mozart's reversals, see Anderson 1938 2:527; 3:1223). In fact, this love of reversals was even manifested in Mozart's musical compositions. In a letter of October 23, 1777, Mozart reports playing for the Dean at the Heiligkreuz Monastery. A monk gave him a theme.

Mozart wrote: "I put it through its paces and in the middle (the fugue was in G minor) I started off in the major key and played something quite lively, though in the same tempo; and after that the theme over again, but this time arseways" ("arschling") (Anderson 1938 2:495).

From the foregoing, it should come as no surprise to learn that Mozart often indulged in expressions of LMIA. For example, the letter to his cousin dated February 28, 1778, closes with: "My greetings to all my friends and whoever doesn't believe me, he can lick me without end, from now to eternity, until I cease to be, that's how long he should lick. I am almost alarmed in this case because I fear that all the 'dreck' will go out of me and there won't be enough for him to eat" (Anderson 1938 2:743).

But surely the best evidence of Mozart's love of LMIA is the fact that he used it as the text for a number of canons. No one but a Mozart perhaps could have conceived and composed canons for three or six voices all singing in succession "Leck mich im Arsch" (cf. K. 231 (382^c) "Leck mich im Arsch," K. 233 (382^d) "Leck mir den Arsch fein recht schön sauber" or the lyrics to K. 560^b "O du eselhafter Martin (Jakob)" which include "Ich scheiss dir aufs Maul...o leck mich doch geschwind im Arsch" and to K. 561 "Bona nox! bist a rechta Ox" which include "scheiss ins Bett.") Thomas Mann in his attempt to describe German character claimed that music, though a "demonic realm," was part of the German soul, a sentiment echoed by Emil Ludwig in his essay "The German Mind" when he said that musicality is a major trait of the German character "without which it is quite impossible to understand them" (1938:258). Mann suggested that Faust should have been musical, should have been a musician. Music, Mann writes, "is calculated order and chaos-breeding irrationality at once" (1946:227).

In this light, I would contend that these obscene canons of Mozart could be perceived as perfect microcosms of German national character. Dirt/filth/feces is expressed or indulged in but only within the rigid and strict confines and rules of a concrete musical structure. Richard Wagner, in his diary *The Brown Book* made a suggestive comment about canons (1980:72). "The common life of the ordinary person is represented in the 'canon': a theme, unaltered, constantly repeated, complementary to itself solely through itself: a character that remains ever constant, so keeping all around it constant." Wagner, to be sure, was speaking of canons in general and not the canons of Mozart, but the insight is a telling one. The endless repetition of LMIA set to music by means of which all participating voices say the same thing though at different times is a musical rendering of the central thesis of this investigation.

Mozart's delight in word play also included the fabrication of fake fecal names. For example, in a letter to his father dated October 17, 1777, Mozart promised to give an account of a concert in his next letter: "A great crowd of the nobility were there: the Duchess Smackbottom, the Countess Makewater, to say nothing of the Princess Dunghill with her two daughters who, however, are already married to the two Princes Potbelly von Pigtail" (Anderson 1938 2:477; cf. Don Cacarello cited earlier.) The idea of constructing such fake names was not invented by Mozart but has a long history in oral and written tradition. Goethe, for instance, around the same time period, wrote a short obscene playlet entitled "Hanswursts Hochzeit oder Der Lauf der Welt: Ein mikrokosmisches Drama." Hanswurst (John Sausage) is the name of a traditional German folk figure (cf. Flögel 1862:186–194). In carnival, he is dressed as a clown and he carries a long leather sausage around his neck. In Goethe's fragmentary account of this character's wedding, one finds among the list of invited wedding guests: Hans Arsch von Rippach; Scheissmatz; Thomas Stinkloch; Blackscheisser, Poet; and such sponsors of the bride as Hosenscheisser and Leckarsch (Goethe 1964:488–496). It should be emphasized that the delight in pseudo-scatological names is a longstanding tradition in Germany. For example, in Wittenwiler's fifteenth-century mock epic The Ring, the hero's name is Bertschi Triefnas (drip nose) and his escutcheon consists of two pitchforks in a dung heap. Three of the peasants have names referring to cow dung: Ochsenkäs [Ox cheese], Fladenranft [Cow pie] and Rindtaisch [Cow dung] while one of the hero's kinswomen is named Jützin Scheissindpluomen [Shit-in-the-flowers] (Wittenwiler 1956:1,35,157).

Goethe did not employ scatological allusions in the fashion of Luther and Mozart. Indeed, in his autobiography, he seems genuinely offended by a joking poem Herder composed and sent him making fun of his name. Herder pretends to ask Goethe to send him letters of Brutus contained in Cicero's letter. "Der von Göttern du stammst, von Gothen oder vom Kothe, Goethe, sende mir sie." [You who stem from the gods, or from the Goths, or from feces, Goethe, send them to me.] Of course, in English translation, some of the punning play on words: Götter [gods], Goethe, Gothen [Goths], and Kothe [feces] is lost (Goethe 1949:366n.1; 1970:339). Goethe's distaste (but considerable interest) in fecal matters is evident in his Italian journey (1786–1788) in which he repeatedly complains about the filth he finds in the streets of nearly every Italian city. His remarks about Venice dated October 1, 1786, are typical: "Today was Sunday, and as I walked about I was struck by the uncleanliness of the streets...The dirt is all the more inexcusable because the city is as designed for cleanliness as any Dutch town...As I walked, I found myself devising sanitary regulations" (1962:64).

What is curiously ironic is that just as Goethe and other German travelers to Italy (cf. Coturnix 1979:78–79) were appalled at what they considered to be inordinately filthy conditions, so English visitors to Germany in the nineteenth century and before made precisely the same criticisms. For example, Samuel Taylor Coleridge wrote short poems entitled "Cologne" and "On My Joyful Departure from the Same City." Speaking of "the body-and-soul-stinking town of Cologne," Coleridge claimed to have counted no less than "two and seventy stenches, All well defined, and several stinks." He even went so far as to suggest that the situation in Cologne was so extreme that it might explain why this city came to be the birthplace of such a famous fragrance as "Eau de Cologne" (Coleridge 1912:477).

For all his concern about cleanliness, Goethe was not totally averse to slinging a bit of fecal mud on occasion. Goethe was annoyed at critic Christoph Friedrich Nicolai who had made fun of his *Sorrows of Werther*. In 1775, Nicolai had published his satire on Werther entitled *Die Freuden des jungen Werthers* [The Joys of young Werther]. Goethe's revenge had obvious scatological overtones. In the celebrated Walpurgis Night scene of Goethe's *Faust*, Part I, Nicolai appears briefly as "Proktophantasmist" which one translator has rendered as "Buttocks-Visionary" (1941:361). More overt is Goethe's poem "Nicolai at Werther's Grave" (Bailey 1972:420–421):

74

A young man, once—I don't know how—
    Succumbed to hypochondri-ow
    And so was duly buried;
Along did come a bel esprit
Who moved his bowels regularly
    As suits a man unharried;

He squatted o'er the grave a while
    Depositing his little pile,
And then pronounced as up he flounced:
    "Ah how could this poor lad himself so slay!
    If he had shat as well as I he'd be alive today!"

This pretty clearly indicates what Goethe thinks of the nature or quality of Nicolai's critique of *Werther*.

There seems little point in citing further examples from German men of letters. The fact is that the anal themes so prominent in German folklore are also to be found among the so-called elite. In sum, anality would appear to be an integral part of general German national character and is not limited to either an occasional peasant or a single exceptional theologian, musician, or poet.

If the Germans do have such a strong anal component in their national character, has it been duly recognized by those who have attempted to define that character? Germans have been interested in national character since long before Germany became a unified nation in 1871. It is probably accurate to say that "the study of national psychology was, indeed, first pursued by German scholars...such as Herder, Humboldt" (Meyer, 1892:242). In 1789, philosopher Immanuel Kant published *Anthropologie in pragmatischer Hinsicht* which included a section devoted to "Der Charakter des Volks" (cf. Moog 1916). After discussing the characteristics of the French and the English, Kant offered a sketch of the significant features of the Germans. Among others, he noted "Fleiss, Reinlichkeit und Sparsamkeit" [Industry, cleanliness, and frugality]. He also claimed that Germans disciplined their children on decency with strictness with a tendency toward "Ordnung und Regel" [order and rule] and that German scholars had an inclination toward classification and pedantry (Kant 1880:247–248). It might be noted that Kant himself had many of these personality traits.

In the two centuries since Kant's brief account, one can find these same traits mentioned again and again as being attributions of German national character. An essay in *Time Magazine* in 1979 quotes a Bonn bureaucrat who describes German qualities as follows: "We are thrifty. Cleanliness and order are still our most valued virtues. We tend to organize everything. Our industriousness is both admired and deplored by foreigners" (Anon. 1979c:32; cf. Hofstätter 1966–67). It is possible that we may be dealing here with stereotype, albeit self-stereotype, rather than national character. But it is safe to say that the image of German national character has proved to be remarkably consistent over time (Nurge 1975:230, 250–254). Numerous writers on Germany, for instance, have commented on how often the phrase "Ordnung muss sein" [There must be order] is repeated in the course of ordinary German conversations (Schaffner 1948:53 cf. Helm 1979). Schalk writes (1971:57) "If there is one word which has traditionally been associated with the German mentality it is the word "Ordnung" (order). One of the highest compliments that can be paid to anyone is to say "Er ist in Ordnung" [he is in order]. When a German wants to settle a dispute, he says, "Ich werde alles in Ordnung bringen" [I will bring everything into order].

Other writers have drawn attention to thriftiness, although several claimed that the trait was more akin to miserliness. Henry Mayhew, writing in the nineteenth century, spoke of the "universal propensity among Germans for saving, as well as stinting themselves of the commonest necessaries of life." He observed further, "The simple fact is, that Germany is a nation of misers" (1864 2:593). Mozart too had commented on this character trait, remarking in 1778, for example, that the "German princes are all skinflints" or in 1790 that "the Frankfurt people are even more stingy than the Viennese" (Anderson 1938 2:750; 3:1406) although Mozart's judgement may have been somewhat influenced by his own poverty and his unsuccessful attempts to obtain adequate financial patronage.

In any case, there is a long list of writings on the subject of German character, some even utilizing folklore (cf. Wähler 1939). A geographer, Georg Ludwig Kriegk, in his *Schriften zur allgemeinen Erdkunde* published in Leipzig in 1840 devoted a substantial chapter of this textbook to "Witz, Scherz und Spott in der geographischen Sprache der Völker" [Joke, Witticism, and Slur in the geographical speech of peoples.]. Around that time appeared other pioneering works in the study of the folklore of and about nations. Representative are J. Venedey, *Die Deutschen und Franzosen nach dem Geiste ihrer Sprachen und Sprüchworter* [The Germans and French according to the spirit of their speech and proverbs] (1842); and Wilhelm Wackernagel, "Die Spottnamen der Volker," which appeared in the *Zeitschrift für Deutsches Alterthum* in 1848. In 1863, the two-volume compilation of Baron Otto von Reinsberg-Düringsfeld, *Internationale Titulaturen,* was published. The first volume treated what peoples said about other peoples while the second volume was limited to what people said about themselves. The trend continued in the twentieth century. In 1918, Wilhelm Wundt published *Die Nationen und ihre Philosophie*, where he attempted to discuss Volkscharakter and Weltanschauung for the Italians, the French, the English, and the Germans. He spoke, for example, of German idealism. A survey of German psychological research undertaken during the Nazi regime remarked that after 1933 characterology became the most favored topic in German psychology (Wyatt and Teuber 1944:231). Typical samples of this enormous literature are: Richard Müller-Freienfels, *The German: His Psychology & Culture: An Inquiry into Folk Character* (1936); Herbert Freudenthal's useful survey "Vorbermerkungen zu einer deutschen Volkscharacterkunde" which was published in the *Zeitschrift für Volkskunde* in 1955; and Gerhard Masur, "Der Nationale Charakter als Problem der Deutschen Geschichte" which appeared in the *Historische Zeitschrift* for 1975. One looks in vain for any mention of anality in any of these scholarly discussions. (It is only occasionally in the popular media that the German penchant for the bathroom is even mentioned, e.g., Vetten 1979.)

Much of the writing about German character has come from non-Germans, stimulated largely by the two world wars. In fact, it is probably fair to say that within the field of national character studies more time and effort has been devoted to the Germans than any other one single national group. However, examination reveals that the vast majority of these investigations are concerned strictly with explaining the rise of Nazism, typically with a discussion of the alleged German authoritarian personality and the German emphasis upon strict obedience to existing authority (cf. Schaffner). Here too, with one or two notable exceptions (e.g., Kecskemeti and Leites 1947–48), no mention is made of possible anal themes in German culture. Anthropologist Robert Lowie, himself of Austrian origin, wrote two books on Germany, but there is no hint of the aspect of German character which is under consideration here.

What is even more curious is that there have been a number of works written on the subject of scatology. While a few have been written by non-Germans, e.g., John G. Bourke, *Scatalogic Rites of All Nations* (1891), Dan Sabbath and Mandel Hall, *End Product: The First Taboo* (1977), and Dominique Laporte, *Histoire de la Merde* (1978), the bulk of the scholarship has been traditionally written in German or by Germans. Representative of this scholarship is Hugo E. Luedecke, "Grundlagen der Skatologie," which appeared in *Anthropophyteia* in 1907, Jean Wegeli, "Das Gesäss in Völkergedanken: Ein Beitrag zur Gluteralerotik" also in *Anthropophyteia* (1912); Franz Maria Feldhaus, *Ka-Pi-Fu und andere verschämte Dinge* (1921)— Ka-Pi-Fu, taken from the initial syllables of the German words for shit, piss, and fart is the standard term among booksellers in Germany for works treating obscenity or scatology; Paul Englisch, *Anrüchiges und Allzumenschliches: Einblicke in das Kapitel PFUI* (1928) and *Das Skatologische Element in Literatur, Kunst und Volksleben* (1928); Ernst Schertel, *Der Erotische Komplex*, Band 1, *Gesäss-Erotik* (1932); a thousand page compendium and discussion entitled *Non Olet oder Die heiteren Tischgespräche des Collofino über den Orbis Cacatus* with a subtitle page which adds *Orbis Cacatus das ist Umständlicher Bericht über Die Beschissene Welt* (1939), the author of whom is identified by Legman (1975:811) as Joseph Feinhals; and more recently Dieter Jürgen Rollfinke's unpublished Johns Hopkins University doctoral dissertation *"Menschliche Kunst: A Study of Scatology in Modern German Literature"* (1977);

79

and Coturnix, *Erbauliche Enzy-Clo-Padie* (1979), a popular cultural history of the bathroom. Most of these works claim to treat scatology in general—even though most of the examples are invariably German, and few suggest that the Germans have any special inclination for scatology.

Even more interesting is the scholarship devoted to defining anal erotic character. If one compares the traits attributed to the Germans—by themselves and by others—to the so-called features of anal erotic characterology as delineated by a number of psychoanalysts going back to Freud himself, one finds a nearly perfect match (cf. Rollfinke 1977:24–26). Freud in his famous 1908 essay claimed that anal erotics are "exceptionally orderly, parsimonious, and obstinate." He further observed that "cleanliness, orderliness, and reliability" appeared to be a "reaction formation against an interest in things that are unclean." Freud's 1908 account of anal character traits is, with the exception of the overt reference to defecation, not all that different from Kant's description of *German* character of 1789. Yet Freud made no reference whatsoever to Germans. Nor did such analysts as Ernest Jones, Karl Abraham, Sandor Ferenczi, and Lou Andreas-Salomé, who wrote on anal erotic character after Freud. No doubt one reason Freud didn't think of Germans in connection with anal erotic character was because he was trying to describe man in general, not just German man. But another reason may have been that German or Austrian writers may not have fully realized that they were writing about themselves. *They* were Austrian-German; their *patients* for the most part were Austrian-German; the *data* they reported was Austrian-German. A fish does not perceive the water in which it swims. In that same 1908 essay, Freud wrote "everyone is familiar with the figure of the 'excreter of ducats'" [*Dukaten-*

Figure 9. Candy *Dukatenscheissers* are still sold in sweet shops.

scheisser]. But English readers, for example, were not familiar with this figure which remains popular in contemporary Germany. Spalding observes that the idea of a mannikin that excretes ducats can be traced back at least to the seventeenth century (1960:509). Candy Dukatenscheissers are still sold in sweet shops. (See figure 9.)

While the money-feces equation is found outside German culture, it is nowhere more explicit than in German folklore. One thinks of the goose that laid the golden egg (Motif B103.2.1, Treasure-laying bird) or the donkey which defecates gold (Motif B103.1.1, Gold-producing ass) or perhaps even German versions of Aarne-Thompson tale type 500, The Name of the Helper. In that folktale, the heroine's parent boasts that the girl can spin straw into gold—is it the straw found in the stable? If so, it would very likely contain animal manure. In this connection, it is curious that the most popular German name of the strange donor figure is Rumpelstilzken, the initial portion of which is etymologically related to the English word "rump" meaning "the hind part of the body." Thus it is a magical backside (whose name is a mystery) which allows feces to be spun into gold. While on the subject of folktales, it is worth mentioning that in a comprehensive study of Aarne-Thompson tale type 480, The Spinning-Women by the Spring, The Kind and the Unkind Girls, based upon more than 900 versions of the tale, the motif of the good heroine rewarded with a "shower of gold" and the bad girl punished by a "shower of pitch" is said to be "a special German development" (Roberts 1958:125). In a typical version from the Schwalm region collected before 1822, each girl's return is announced by a rooster: "Unser goldenes Mädchen kommt" [Our golden girl comes] and "Unser dreckiges Mädchen kommt" [Our filthy girl comes] (Bolte and Polivka 1913:208).

Here we can see that what may be an oicotype or local form of one single folktale is in all probability related to a definite, more general cultural feature. But the feces–gold equation in Germany does not depend upon any one example. One could cite the case of Frederick William I (1688-1740), father of Frederick the Great. He is reported to have written marginalia on requests for money. In one instance, he declined a request as follows (Waite 1977:254):

| Eure Bitte kann ich nicht gewähren. | Your request I cannot grant. |
| Ich habe hunderttausend Mann zu ernähren. | I have 100,000 men to feed. |

| Gold kann ich nicht scheissen. | I cannot shit gold. |
| Friedrich Wilhelm, König in Preussen. | Frederick William, King of Prussia. |

A more modern example of the equation is found in the form of a joking question: "Wie verhält sich die Borse zu einem Abort?" [How is the stock exchange like a bathroom?] "Auf der Borse fallen zuerst die Papiere und dann kommt der Krach, auf dem Abort gibt es zuerst einen Krach und dann erst fallen die Papiere" [At the exchange, first the paper falls and then comes the crash; in the bathroom, first comes a crash and then the paper falls] (Polsterer 1908:171; cf. Luedecke 1907:325). Even the denial that feces is gold tends to underscore the existence of the symbolic equation. An example of "Nachttopf-Verse" or chamberpot poetry (Luedecke 1907:327) illustrates this:

| Das Bächlein rauscht, der Donner rollt, | The stream rushes, the thunder rolls, |
| Was darin steckt, ist kein Gold. | What lies therein isn't gold. |

One of the many proverbs based upon the equation is: "Geld ist Dreck, aber Dreck is kein Geld" [Money is shit, but shit is not money] (Wander 1964 1:1482).

The ubiquitousness of the gold–feces equation in German folklore presumably helped Freud to discover or delineate anal erotic character. The equation is prominently featured in Freud and Oppenheim's *Dreams in Folklore,* a book whose main point is that many of the symbolic interpretations employed by psychoanalysts have already been articulated in traditional folktales. One section of this important work treats penis symbolism (1958:26-36) while another, longer, section discusses feces symbolism (1958:36-65). The relative weight given by Freud and Oppenheim to examples of anal material as opposed to genital items supports the view discussed earlier of the preference of Germans for anal over sexual topics. It was surely appropriate that it was Freud who wrote the introduction to the German translation in 1913 of Bourke's *Scatologic Rites of All Nations*.

In this context, one cannot help but recall one of Freud's own dreams that he analyzes in some detail in *The Interpretation of Dreams* (1938:440-442; cf. Grinstein's (1968:423-446) extended discussion of this "Open-Air Closet" dream). In the dream, Freud sees "something like an open-air latrine; a very long bench at the end of which is a wide aperture. The whole of its back edge is thickly covered with little heaps of excrement of all sizes and degrees of freshness...I urinate upon the bench; a long stream of urine rinses everything clean, the patches of excrement come off easily and fall into the opening." Freud asks why did he experience no disgust in this dream? Upon reflection, he thought of Hercules' cleansing of the Augean stables and he identified himself with the mythological hero. Implied also is a parallel with psychoanalysis itself insofar as he through the force of his urine is able to clean up a "disgusting" aspect of the human condition. What is most significant is that Freud perceived his life's work in terms of an outhouse metaphor and that he saw himself as a hero who fearlessly used his own body products to eliminate the filth left by others. One is tempted to speculate about Freud's choice of the term "psychoanalysis" to represent his approach to the human mind. For as Menninger (1943:181) reminds us, the root stem of analyzing is *anal* from a Greek root *ana* meaning back. The basic meanings of analysis seem to include "back" and "unloosing" with a sense of decomposing something. Thus "psychoanalysis" would be a kind of mental backward releasing (reconstructing crucial childhood events back in the indi-

vidual's past) and it might be fair to say that part of the therapeutic process involves flushing "dirt" out of a patient's head!

Whatever the merits of the above musings on the word
"psychoanalysis," it does seem clear that the various refine-
ments of anal erotic characterology appear to be applicable to
Germans. For example, Karl Abraham's paper "Contributions
to the Theory of Anal Character" of 1921 notes "Pleasure in
indexing and classifying, in compiling lists and statistical sum-
maries, in drawing up programmes and regulating work by
time-sheets, is well known to be an expression of the anal
character" (1953:377, 388). The German penchant for elaborate indexing and encyclopedic compilations is to be found in
a wide variety of academic disciplines. Abraham also commented on the distinction between the pleasure of holding
back the excreta and of evacuating it. He maintained that "anal
character" sometimes led individuals to postpone actions or to
store up materials collected until finally letting everything go
(or housecleaning) in one big blast. It occurs to me that the
very structure of German sentences would tend to support this
philosophy. A host of nouns and adjectival phrases are built up
until finally a crucial verb mercifully appears at the end of the
sentence to release all the semantic meaning which has ac-
crued. Such linguistic structure might appropriately be construed as metaphorically supporting the postponement principle. (One wonders if an analogy to the verb occurring at the
end of most German sentences is the custom of placing the
table of contents of a book at the end rather than at the
beginning. It is only by looking at the back of the book—like
the end of a sentence—that one is able to quickly discover
what the book is about.)

This is not the place to rehearse the vast literature devoted to anal erotic character; much of the recent work is experimental and critical in nature (Kubie 1937; Landauer 1939; Huschka 1942; Merrill 1951; Buckle 1953; Prugh 1954; Beloff 1957; Heimann 1962; Wisdom 1966; Bishop 1967; Ross, Hirt and Kurtz 1968; Centers 1969; Hermand 1971; Kline 1972; and Hill 1976). I would observe only that to my knowledge none of the published literature makes any specific reference to German personality traits. I should mention that the theory does involve the concept of sublimation. Ferenczi, for example, brilliantly traced the development in children of an evolving interest in mud, modeling clay, and a host of successively drier materials: sand, pebbles, shells, marbles, as well as the concept of reaction formation in which an individual intensely dislikes dirt, disorder, and waste. In addition, there is the distinction between anal-retention (the hoarding, miserly type) and anal ejection. Note, too, that *Besitz*, possession, derives from the word for sit (Ferenczi 1956:275n.3).

The German concern for cleanliness would be a prime example of reaction formation in terms of standard anal erotic character theory. And no one can doubt the German's obsession with cleanliness. For example, a rhyming maxim often painted on wood and hung as a motto in a hall or in the kitchen is (Sidgwick 1912:134):

Wie die Küche so das Haus, As the kitchen so the house
Reinlich drinnen, reinlich draus Clean therein, clean throughout

The notion of clean, *'rein,'* also is common in German literature. Nietzsche extols his "instinct for cleanliness" claiming that it was for him the presupposition of his existence. "My whole *Zarathustra* is a dithyramb on solitude or, if I have been understood, on *cleanliness''* (Kaufmann 1968:689-690).

Nietzsche went so far as to say "But psychology is almost the measure of the *cleanliness* or *uncleanliness* of a race....What is called 'deep' in Germany is precisely this instinctive uncleanliness in relation to oneself" (Kaufmann 1968:778).

Wolff (1970–1971), for example, thoroughly documents the centrality of 'rein' in Rilke's poetry although he makes no mention of the possible underlying anal erotic significance of such usage. What we have in effect is that writers on German national character have amply documented the existence of such traits as orderliness and cleanliness, but they have utterly failed to relate these traits to the psychoanalytic theory of anal erotic character. By the same token, psychoanalytic writers on anal erotic character have seemingly neglected to apply the theory to German national character, possibly because so many of these writers were German or Austrian. Admittedly there are occasional exceptions.

Kenneth Burke (1963:378-382) does call our attention to the importance of clean gold in Wagner's *Das Rheingold,* reminding us that Wagner specifically puns on "Rheingold" and "reines Gold" in the lament of the Rhine maidens at the close of the opera. It would make perfect sense for a German opera imbued with nationalistic sentiment to celebrate the possession of clean gold—*Pecunia non olet!* Burke astutely observes that when Alberich gains control over the gold, he does so by renouncing love, "that is, he chooses the fecal, in rejecting the sexual," an esthetic choice totally consistent with the ethos of German culture. Burke, however, is interested in demonstrating the nature of catharsis in literature rather than defining German character per se.

Folklorist Gershon Legman, one of the few scholars, to have written on the German's love of scatology, offers an explanation of the cleanliness trait along Freudian lines: Speaking of national preferences in jokes, Legman observes (1958:15):

> Germans and the Dutch, for example, are obviously far more susceptible to scatology in humor than to any other theme. This is doubtless a reaction to excessively strict and early toilet-training, and general rigidity and compulsiveness in the Teutonic upbringing and character, and is an open release for the resultant 'cleanliness complex' in later life, common in all Anglo-Saxon cultures. A clever joke-teller can bring the usual German audience to quite a high pitch of screaming entertainment, rolling out of their seats, and so forth, just by *preparing* to tell a joke of which the inevitable punch-line must include the word 'shit' (sometimes built up to the reduplicative 'scheissdreck') without ever even beginning the joke.

I might add that in German culture not only does defecation produce humor, but, according to one proverbial expression (Spalding 1974:1373), humor can on occasion cause an act of defecation: "vor Lachen in die Hosen machen" [to shit in one's pants from laughing].

I would agree that if we wish to explore the possibility that German national character may be illuminated through recourse to anal erotic traits, we need to examine the critical details of toilet training. Is German toilet training 'excessively strict and early' and does it differ materially from toilet training practiced, say, among other Western European nations?

In an important cross-cultural study of the possible relationships between child training generally and adult personality, Whiting and Child report (1953:74), "The median estimate for the beginning age of serious toilet training falls at the age of two. Slightly over half of the primitive societies (14 out of 25) begin toilet training somewhere between the ages of one and a half and two and a half." The range ran essentially from six months to five years. On the basis of studies of the neuromuscular development of infants (presumably American), one re-searcher concluded that "toilet training may start as early as 8 months, more usually after 15 months" (Huschka 1942:304-305). Huschka in her report of a study of bowel training in a group of problem children accepted the period from 18 months to 24 months as adequate, and considered training completed before the child was 18 months old to be coercive (1942:305). A 1974 American primer entitled *Toilet Training in Less Than a Day* claims that a child of 20 months is capable of being toilet-trained and that in view of variable rates of physical and mental development, some children may be ready at a slightly earlier age, for example, 18 months (Azrin and Foxx, 1974:43). It is clear that there is considerable variation and difference of opinion as to precisely when a child is deemed to be toilet trainable, but in view of the comparative data, which suggest that a cross-cultural norm for the beginning of toilet training is roughly 24 months with the lower minimum in American culture of 18 months (without taking ethnic differences in American society into account), we may now turn to German custom.

Not many social scientists have bothered to record accurate toilet training data, but there is some. In *Postwar Germans: An Anthropologist's Account,* published in 1948, we find the following report: "Since toilet training habits are important in the emotional experiences of the child, it is interesting to note how early the child is conditioned in German family life. Among all classes, toilet training begins when the infant is about five months old. There is a belief among German mothers that the child should be completely 'housebroken' by the time it is a year old" (Rodnick 1948:18). Similarly, a comprehensive study of cleanliness training in a German Swiss canton reported that toilet training might begin as early as 5 months (Fuchs 1969:90, 106). A 1964 description of a nursery in a southwest German village confirms the continued concern with early toilet training. Before entering kindergarten at age three or four, children may attend the village nursery. Some come as early as six weeks after birth. According to the account,

> In the middle of the play area, strung out in a ragged column, were seven children perched on pots. They were quiet, contented, and apparently waiting for something to happen....The daily routine begins before lunch. The children are delivered between 11:00 and noon, and since they are sheduled for a nap, toilet training begins immediately. After this session they are given a snack, allowed to play for a few minutes, and put to bed. For the next two hours they remain in bed, to sleep or at least rest. At 3:00 P.M. they are allowed to get up. The babies are cleaned, the older ones put on the pot again and given plenty of time to succeed (Warren 1967:41-42).

All right, so the Germans do seem to start toilet training a bit early, one may say, but what evidence is there for believing there is any linkage between toilet training and the standard German character traits of order and cleanliness? Are we obliged to simply accept the self-serving assertions of psychoanalysts? The answer is that folklore holds the key. I believe I can demonstrate that data derived from folklore can be adduced to provide prima facie evidence for the association between toilet training and the German concern for order and cleanliness. In a railroad station in Binz auf Rügen in 1902, the following revealing latrinalia couplet was found. In fact, it is widely known in Germany (Luedecke 1907:319; cf. Praetorius 1911:422; Krotus 1970:15):

Wer hier will nach der Ordnung leben,
der scheiss ins Loch und nicht daneben!

He who wants to live according to order
should shit into the hole and not beside it.

In a variant (Anon. 1912:506), "Reinlichkeit ist's halbes Leben; Scheiss in's Loch und nicht daneben." [Cleanliness is half of life, shit in the hole and not beside it.] An analogous folk rhyme makes the issue a matter of national pride (Vetten 1979 [49]:131; cf. Borneman 1973:371):

Meine Herren und Damen	Ladies and Gentlemen
machen Sie nicht auf den Rahmen	don't do it on the rim,
machen Sie in die Mitte,	do it in the middle
das ist deutsche Sitte.	that is German custom.

This connection between the concern for cleanliness and toilet training is not just a psychoanalytic construct. Rather it is an association proclaimed openly in German folklore. Freud himself might have been familiar with such folklore.

Of course, not everyone succeeds in shitting in the hole, but one need not necessarily apologize for this lack of order (Waldheim 1910:406):

Ich hab hier auf das Brett geschissen	I have shit here on the board
wer sich reinsetzt den lass ich	To whoever sits down in it, I send
grüssen.	greetings.

Evidence from German folklore also suggests that defecating in the wrong place may result in punishment. For example, one folk term for sty (on the eye) is 'Wegscheisser' [way shitter] which refers to the belief that defecating on a public path will cause a sty to appear (Hand 1980:211). It is curious that even in English a sty can be an inflammatory swelling on an eyelid or a filthy place such as a pig pen.)

The important theoretical point here is that so-called anal erotic character traits are specifically linked to toilet activities in German folklore (as opposed to psychoanalytic theory).

Consider the first two stanzas of a folksong entitled "Das Lied von der Reinlichkeit" (The song of Cleanliness) collected at a Gymnasium school party in Augsburg in 1894 (Heimpel, 1912:502, reprinted in Englisch, 1928b:189-191):

Um die Reinlichkeit zu fördern,	In order to advance the cause of cleanliness,
juchheidi, juchheida,	Hurray, Hurrah
Ist vor allem zu erörtern,	It is necessary above all else to discuss
juchheidi, heida,	Hurray, rah,
Wie, womit, wozu and wann	How, with what, to what end, and when
Man sich reinlich putzen kann.	One can scrub oneself clean
Juchheidi, heidi, heida,	Hurray, ray rah, hurray, hurrah
juchheidi, juchheida	Hurray, ray, rah, hurray, rah
Juchheidi, heidi, heida,	
juchheidi, heida!	
Schon in seinen Kinderjahren	Already in childhood
juchheidi, juchheida,	Hurray, Hurrah,
Hat ein jeder wohl erfahren,	Everyone has learned well,
juchheidi, heida,	Hurray, rah,
Dass man von dem Stuhlgang her	That one comes back from going to stool
Nicht so reinlich wie vorher.	Not as clean as before.
Juchheidi, heidi, heida,	Hurray, ray, rah, hurray, hurrah
juchheidi, juchheida	Hurray, ray, rah, Hurray, rah.
Juchheidi, heidi, heida,	
juchheidi, heida!	

The song continues for fifteen more stanzas describing in some detail the various difficulties encountered in cleaning one's posterior after defecating, ending with a passionate plea: "Männer, Greise, Weiber, Kinder, Haltet reinlich Eure Hinter!" [Men, old men, women, children, Keep your backside clean!]

Traits other than cleanliness are also mentioned in German folklore. For example, a riddle provides a partial definition of thriftiness (Krauss and Reiskel, 1905:47):

Welche Sparsamkeit ist die unverschämteste?
Which thriftiness is the most shameful?

Wenn man in das Arschwischpapier ein Loch macht, um sich mit
dem Finger den Arsch auszuwischen und das Papier wieder
aufhebt.
When a person makes a hole in the toilet paper to wipe his ass with
his finger and keeps the paper to use again.

Whatever one may think of the hypothetical linkage between
severe or early toilet training and so-called anal erotic character traits in adulthood, I believe there is another distinctive
feature of infantile conditioning which may be just as significant as the date of the onset of toilet training. For even if toilet
training is initiated at the age of one year or earlier, there is,
after all, a period of some length of time *before* formal training
begins, and it is my contention that this early period may also
be critical with respect to the formation of adult personality.
The difficulty, frankly, in seeking a correlation between earliest
infant care and adult personality is the disgraceful lack of
relevant ethnographic data. Few observers have recorded the
details and minutiae of the first days, weeks, and months of an
infant's existence. This lacuna is, of course, true for most cultures. Nevertheless, several reports exist which, if they are
representative, may greatly assist us in determining the nature
of German infant care in centuries past.

One of the widespread practices in Germany as elsewhere
in Europe (and for that matter in cultures in many parts of the
world) was swaddling. (For a discussion of the distribution and
antiquity of swaddling, see Dennis 1940:208-211; Hudson and
Phillips 1968; cf. de Mause 1975:37-38.) Swaddling consists of
wrapping a baby in long strips of cloth. The infant is normally
rendered immobile by this bandaging-like process, although

techniques vary so that in some cases the infant's upper limbs are left free.

It was Rousseau who argued forcibly against the custom of swaddling infants. In *Émile* (1762), Rousseau criticized the practice on philosophical grounds. His basic premise, expressed in the opening sentence, was "Everything is good as it comes from the hands of the Author of Nature; but everything degenerates in the hands of man." Rousseau cited swaddling as an extreme instance of human bondage. "Civilized man is born, lives, and dies in a state of slavery. At his birth he is stitched in swaddling-clothes; at his death he is nailed in his coffin; and as long as he preserves the human form he is fettered by our institutions." Rousseau calls swaddling an "unreasonable" and "unnatural" custom. He is quite clear in what he recommends as appropriate infant care: "Do not suffer the child to be restrained by caps, bands, and swaddling-clothes; but let him have gowns flowing and loose, and which leave all his limbs at liberty, not so heavy as to hinder his movements, nor so warm as to prevent him from feeling the impression of the air . . . Place the child in a wide cradle, well cushioned, where he can move at his ease and without danger. When he begins to grow strong, let him creep about the room and develop his little limbs, by giving them exercise; you will see him gain in strength day by day. Compare him with a child of the same age who has been tightly confined in swaddling-clothes, and you will be astonished at the difference in their progress." Rousseau also recommended that "Children should be bathed frequently" (Rousseau 1906:1, 10, 24-25).

In modern times, it has been Geoffrey Gorer who called attention to the possible influence swaddling might have on the development of adult personality, specifically among Russians. His so-called "swaddling hypothesis," first proposed in 1949 was not received with equal enthusiasm by all anthropologists. Many considered it the ultimate in absurdist Freudian reductionism. Some, however, were intrigued by it. Ruth Benedict wrote a brief essay (1949) entitled "Child Rearing in Certain European Countries" in which she used Gorer's hypothesis as the basis of comparative remarks. She suggested an important difference between Russian and Polish swaddling, for example. Whereas Russian informants indicated that the infant was swaddled to keep it from destroying itself (without swaddling, an infant would tear its ears off or break its legs), Polish informants regarded the infant as fragile rather than violent. Thus the Polish infant was swaddled to "harden" it. Benedict in this imaginative way tried to show that it was not necessarily swaddling per se which produced national characteristics, but only that parental attitudes toward infants were reflected in the rationales given for swaddling and further that these different parental attitudes were indicative of significant distinctions in national character. All this notwithstanding, it is fair to say that the general reaction to the swaddling hypothesis was at best mixed, with most scholars remaining highly skeptical. (For a sample of the academic responses to Gorer's views, see Mead 1954; and Kluckhohn 1962:210-243.)

From the present perspective, one serious deficiency in the swaddling hypothesis was the total lack of attention paid to details of toilet training and sphincter control (cf. Greenacre 1944:214). The issue in these terms is thus not so much whether an infant was swaddled, but how often the swaddling was changed and the infant bathed. Unfortunately, what few accounts of swaddling there are rarely make any mention of this facet of early infant care. One exception is Charlotte Gower

Chapman in her study of a Sicilian village in 1928. She bothered to record that "Small babies are swaddled for warmth and to make their legs grow straight. The wrappings are changed three times a day" (1971:25). If we had more detailed accounts of Polish swaddling with respect to how often the swaddling clothes were changed, we might be in a better position to speculate on the possible significance of a startling Polish folk metaphor for a person's place in the world as "Mruvka v'guvnie"; literally "an ant in a pile of shit" (Stein 1978:41). A German idiom paints a comparable picture. "Dastehen wie das Kind beim Dreck" [to be like a child in shit] suggests a state of being utterly helpless (Spalding 1960:496), but the situation is evidently not truly hopeless if one believes that "aus beschissenen Kindern werden auch Leut" [from shitty children will one day come people] (Spalding 1955:266).

Let us now turn to some available accounts of German infant care which may be relevant to the present investigation. Henry Mayhew who is perhaps best known for his painstaking descriptions of urban life in mid-nineteenth-century London also spent time in Germany. On the basis of five years' residence and study (1864:2:103), Mayhew published *German Life and Manners* in two volumes in 1864. Included in his careful account is the following:

"Immediately after birth, the poor babe is fed, for the twenty-four hours at least, upon herb-tea and sugar water, for it is not allowed to taste a drop of milk during that time; nor is it permitted to sleep with its mother, or nurse, at night, but is stowed away, generally, in a small clothes-basket, with a pillow for its bed, after the wretched new-born little thing has been wound up in, Heaven knows how many ells of bandages, from the feet right, and tight, up to the neck; as if it were intended to be embalmed as a mummy, and God Almighty had never designed it to have the free use of its

muscles and limbs. In its swaddled state a new-born babe looks as
if it were one of the young Caryatides with a human head on a
shapeless trunk of stone."

The newborn infant's clothing consists of a coarse linen shirt,
the bandages, and a little colored-jacket

> In which state it is stuffed into a "Kissen" (cushion) or "Steck-bett"
> as it is expressively called on the Rhine (literally the *bed* into which
> new-born children are *stuck*), after the manner of a watch into a
> watch-pocket, and not half so comfortably as a young kangaroo in
> the pouch of its mother. These swaddled infants are called in
> Germany *Wickel-kinder.''*

Mayhew goes on to describe the state of such infants in more
detail:

> "In Germany, however, babies are loathsome, foetid things—rank
> with the sour black pap or goat's milk upon which they have been
> fed, and offensive to the last degree with the excreta that are kept
> bound up within their swaddling clothes for *twelve hours* at a time
> [The emphasis on twelve hours is Mayhew's, not mine]. Then the
> heads of the poor things are never washed, and are like the rind of
> Stilton cheese, with the dirt encrusted upon the skull, till the hair
> differs from the exquisite flossy tresses of our own countrywomen's
> children as widely as the bristles on a pig's back differ from the
> gossamer-like filaments of the silkworm."

Mayhew concludes: "The swaddling-clothes and nightcaps
are continued with infants until they are nearly six months old"
(Mayhew 1864 1:490–494).

Mayhew's striking account is confirmed by other observers.
A woman who had also spent five years in Germany wrote an
essay on "Female Education in Germany," which appeared in
Cornhill Magazine in 1867. She included the following description:

A German baby is a piteous object; it is pinioned and bound up like a mummy in yards of bandages, which are unfolded once (at the outside twice) a day; it is never bathed, but I suppose is sometimes washed in some occult manner. Its head is never touched with soap and water until it is eight or ten months old, when the fine skull-cap of encrusted dirt which it has by that time obtained is removed by application of various unguents. Many German ladies have assured me that the fine heads of hair one so often sees in Germany are entirely owing to this skull-cap. (Anon. 1867:365)

Still another writer, an Englishwoman of German parentage, wrote a book entitled *Home Life in Germany* at the beginning of the twentieth century. She offered the following account of infant life:

"When the baby has come it is not allowed out of doors for weeks. Air and sunlight are considered dangerous at first, and so is soap and even an immoderate use of water. For eight weeks it lies day and night in the *Steckkissen,* a long bag that confines its legs and body but not its arms. The bag is lined with wadding, and a German nurse, who was showing me one with great pride, assured me that while a child's bones were soft it was not safe to lift it in any other way. These bags are comparatively modern, and have succeeded the swaddling clothes still used in some parts of Germany. They are bandages wrapping the child round like a mummy, and imprisoning its arms as well as its legs. A German doctor told me that as these *Wickelkinder* had never known freedom they did not miss it; but he seemed to approve of the modern compromise that leaves the upper limbs some power of movement. (Sidgwick 1912:7–8)

One wonders how far back in time swaddling was practiced in Germany. The evidence available from representations in art suggest considerable antiquity for the custom. From depictions of a swaddled Jesus to toy swaddled dolls, one can document the existence of swaddling in Germany for several centuries at least (Cf. Müllerheim 1904:103–123).

While one must always be wary of the bias that may creep into the accounts of one culture by natives of another, the consistency of the above three independent descriptions of early infant care in Germany suggests accuracy. Mayhew in particular was struck by the swaddling practice he observed, so much so that he used the *Wickelkind* image as a kind of recurring leitmotif in his ethnography, implying that it was a useful metaphor for German personality—and he did this nearly a century before Gorer proposed his swaddling hypothesis! He hinted that the government treats the German citizenry "as though they were literally the *children* of the Fatherland: to deal with them, indeed, as the German nurses do with newly-born infants—bind the poor things in no end of swaddling clothes, till they have not the power to move either hand or foot, as if the Almighty had never intended them to have the least liberty." Mayhew also perceives the German educational system as an extension of swaddling:

> "In Germany, however, the young are trained to such a respect, if not reverence, for the pedagogue, that your real Deutscher would sooner think of questioning the truth of Revelation than of doubting the rules he has learnt of the schoolmaster or the critics. Hence, he begins life trammelled, like a *Wickel-kind*, with all kind of aesthetical, rhetorical, and philosophical bandages, in the shape of scholastic dogmata; and consequently, grows up with his mental functions crippled to such an extent with formulae that he is unable to run alone for the rest of his days. (Mayhew 1864 2:640–641; 1:541)

It is instructive to compare Mayhew's metaphorical account of what he sees as the restrictive nature of German personality with a twentieth-century study written by a German psychologist. In *The German: His Psychology & Culture: An Inquiry into Folk Character*, first published in 1922, Müller-Freienfels makes a special point of describing what he termed the "voluntary acceptance of self-imposed restraint." In his extended discussion of the "free acceptance of coercion" and "the voluntary binding of self," he makes absolutely no reference whatsoever to the custom of swaddling. However, if he is correct in labeling the phenomenon he calls the "German's voluntary acceptance of restraint," this could well be a reflection of—if not a result of—infant swaddling. Müller-Freienfels tends to describe rather than explain what he means: "The German really feels comfortable only when he organizes some sort of association with statutes, paragraphs, board of directors, membership badges, and many other such visible signs of his being bound down. This form of social life dominated by the principle of voluntary acceptance of blind discipline is something expressly German and arises quite organically from the German temper of mind. The need for statutory control and regulation accrues from a certain inability for self-guidance" (1936:138–140, 147–149, 227; for a similar argument linking swaddling among Slovak-Americans to adult feelings of resignation to life and deference to external authority, see Stein 1978).

Thomas Mann in his essay "Germany and the Germans," written in the aftermath of World War II, suggested that perhaps the most notable quality of the Germans is what he termed "inwardness." He found that term difficult to define. Swaddling, one could well argue, might account for such a quality. An infant tightly bound has little opportunity for extensive interaction with the external world and can not do much else than turn inward. Referring to the German concept of liberty, in a political sense, Mann asks, "Why must the German urge for liberty always be tantamount to inner enslavement?" (Mann

1946:223–241). Again, swaddling may in part illuminate such a feeling of enslavement.

In the light of this discussion, it is interesting that two astute students of German character have called attention to the importance of metaphors concerning hindrances to free movement. One set of such metaphors involves the verb *binden*.

> A "Bindung" can mean a (desired or undesired) loss of freedom, or an attachment. To acknowledge a service is to be "verbunden." A "Bund" is something in the nature of a league...Closely related to "binden" is "fesseln" (to shackle)... A thrilling novel is "fesselnd."... Other expressions describing deprivations of any kind as hindrances to movement are "in die Enge getrieben werden," "eingekreist werden."... Similarly, indulgences may be described by looseness or loosening of external restraints on movements, e.g., "sich aus der Umklammerung befreien," "Bewegungsfreiheit," "uneingeschränkt," "Erlösung." (Kecskemeti and Leites 1947:152)

However, despite these writers' recognition of the anal character of Germans, they offer no real explanation for the apparent predilection for such metaphors. I submit that swaddling could explain in part the popularity of this type of root metaphor. Lewin (1936:271) also drew attention to the relative lack of space or free movement for German children as compared with American children.

I believe Mayhew was on the right track and that he correctly anticipated psychoanalytic theory which postulates a connection or correlation between infant care and adult personality. The continued use of the German expression "Der ist falsch gewickelt" [he was swaddled wrongly] suggesting that a misguided individual was damaged as an infant through poor child care hints that the folk themselves may have sensed the connection between infant care and adult personality. One might suppose, for example, that the important twentieth-century German notion of Lebensraum (living space) might reflect something more than political history or the particularities of the personality of Hitler. Lebensraum may conceivably go back to the painful discomfort of severe swaddling techniques. As an infant seeks more "living space," so adults in the same culture might find great appeal in a concept that offered the nation (and its citizens) a chance to move around and spread out.

The specifics of German swaddling, in which the infant is left in contact with its own feces, may also be germane. One recalls, for example, the longstanding custom of building fortifications of feces. As the swaddling infant is "surrounded" by feces (which perhaps is perceived as keeping powerful adult figures away) so the adult might feel protected by building walls of manure. Even more persuasive is the possibility of understanding the curious pleasure of repeatedly "shitting in bed" and "shitting in pants," noted by Mozart and celebrated so often in folk poetry. This could explain the popularity of children's rhymes about defecating in trousers or the verses which spoke of "Shit on [or behind] the sofa cushion." Related to this is a variant of the "Das Leben ist wie. . ." series discussed earlier in this essay. Popular in Frankfurt in the 1960s was "Das Leben ist wie ein Kindernachthemd: Kurz und beschissen" [Life is like a child's nightshirt—short and shitty]. In effect, this single piece of folklore has aptly summed up the entire swaddling hypothesis proposed here!

There is no contradiction between allowing an infant to remain immersed in his own feces and urine on the one hand, and insisting upon early potty training on the other. One of Nietzsche's epigrams in *Beyond Good and Evil* sums up the

102

apparent paradox: "The disgust with dirt can be so great that it keeps us from cleaning ourselves" (Kaufmann 1968:276). A German mother, under the influence of reaction formation, simply would not want to deal with her infant's feces. So initially, she would resort to swaddling with a minimum amount of changing, and later, but as early as possible, she would begin to toilet train the infant. All these actions are consistent with a desire to avoid close contact with feces. Yet reaction formation may not always be entirely successful. We understand that this notion depends upon the idea of compensating for one urge by indulging in its opposite. So an individual fixated upon dirt becomes compulsively clean—in the same way as a would-be alcoholic becomes a champion of temperance or a would-be devotee of pornography becomes a self-appointed film or library censor. But the original, initiating impulse is not always eliminated. So in German culture, I suspect we have a double image of "clean and dirty" occurring simultaneously. The German may pay lip service to cleanliness, but deep down he continues to revel in dirt.

One could not find a more succinct codification of the distinction between manifest and latent content than the proverbial "Aussen hui! Innen pfui!" popular in both the nineteenth and twentieth centuries (Spalding 1974:1378), which might be rendered in English as "Outside clean; Inside dirty." The recognition of the hypocrisy of reaction formation is equally evident in a version from Berlin "Oben hui, unten pfui" which one translator gives as "On top all spry, below, oh fie." Another version from Bavaria is even more forthright: "Oben beglissen, unten beschissen," that is, "above shining, below beshat" (Abraham 1953:388n.1). A German Wellerism variant on "All that glitters is not gold" makes much the same point, in addition to confirming the well-known gold-feces symbolic equation. "Es ist nicht alles Gold, was glänzt! sagte der Herr— da war er in einen Haufen Kleinkinderscheisse getreten" [All is not gold that glistens, said the man as he stepped into a pile of baby shit] (Berliner 1910:379).

The German fascination with cleanliness and dirt also finds expression in art and sculpture. For example, the urge to get rid of polluting dirt may account for the presence of gargoyles on medieval churches. Gargoyles provided an outlet for the rainwater which periodically cleansed the exterior of the church. In Germany, the gargoyles sometimes took the form of buttocks. A classic instance is the Catholic cathedral in Frei- burg in Breisgau in which a bent-over figure's protruding anus provides the necessary waterspout (Rollfinke 1977:27).

Survey data supports the "clean-dirty" discrepancy. In a lengthy report published in 1976 entitled "Wie sauber sind die Deutschen?" [How clean are the Germans?], it was discovered that although Germans thought of themselves as a very clean people—cleanliness along with industriousness and orderli- ness were high-ranking traits of the self-stereotype, the facts of daily hygiene proved otherwise (Anon. 1976:126–144). The majority of adults questioned in polls in 1964 and 1975 took a bath only once a week. (One can't help recalling the nine- teenth-century accounts which specifically commented on the rarity of infant bathing.) In one sample, only 11 percent owned their own toothbrush. A *Newsweek* report indicated that a 1975 survey found that 43 percent of all Germans never brush their teeth (cf. Schalk, 1971:56). In the 1964 poll, 12 percent changed underwear daily, 52 percent changed every second or third day, while 31 percent wore the same underwear for more than a week (Anon. 1976:130). More than a century ago,

Mayhew observed that undergarments were changed but once a month (1864 1:215).

All this tends to support the claim that the combination of clean and dirty: clean exterior–dirty interior, or clean form and dirty content—is very much a part of German national character. Mozart, as noted earlier, provided a musical metaphor for this paradox by composing strict canons on the "Leck mich im Arsch" text. Erich Kahler in his 1974 book *The Germans* describes the issue in more general philosophical terms: "As in philosophy, so now in literature, the German mind had to reconcile two opposing tendencies, one giving free rein to emotion and inspiration, the other prescribing rational discipline" (1974:250). But Kahler says absolutely nothing about anal characteristics. He, like other German intellectuals, knows about Freud, but he chooses to reject Freudian analysis a priori—one would think a good German would reject it a posteriori! In view of the overwhelming folklore data sampled in the present investigation—data for the most part readily available in print—one wonders how many more book-length studies of Germany, especially those purporting to treat German personality, will continue to totally ignore this critical facet of German character.

It is one thing to assert that the German preoccupation with scatological themes is essential to a fuller understanding of German culture; it is quite another to demonstrate this. The point is that studies of national character are not or should not be ends in themselves. They are merely tools to aid us in comprehending the subtleties of whatever people or culture we wish to know better. For this reason, I should like to conclude this essay by considering selected aspects of German culture, e.g., food preferences, the development of printing, and anti-Semitism. These would appear to be totally disparate topics, but I hope to show that the analysis of German national character presented here makes all these subjects part of the same general pattern. Anthropologists holding a holistic view of cultures are accustomed to assuming that a cultural pattern may be all-pervasive, manifesting itself in an infinite and bewildering variety of cultural traits ranging from culinary habits to ideological systems. With such a view, the overall pattern of the whole may be found in any and every constituent part. This essay itself is intended to be a demonstration of such cultural consistency. It is for the reader to judge whether these representative elements of German culture can be seen in a new light.

There can be no question that the Germans typically think of the end product of eating, but it is also true that both facets of the digestive process are frequently linked. In a letter written on June 6, 1791, Mozart wrote to his wife who was taking the cure at Baden, "I am delighted that you have a good appetite—but whoever gorges a lot, must also shit a lot—no, walk a lot, I mean.... Listen, I want to whisper something in your ear—and you in mine... at last we say: 'It is all about Plumpi-Strumpi—'" (Anderson, 1938 3:1416). The meaning of the non-sense word "Plumpi" is not entirely clear, but it may well be related to the onomatopoeic root used in slang terms for open-air defecation, e.g., Plumpsklo, Plumpsabe, Plumpsdings-bums, etc. (See Borneman 1971:72.12). Johann Georg Hamann (1730–1788), a contemporary of Herder and Kant, often referred to as the Magus (wise man) of the North once remarked in a letter written to a woman in 1787: "It is noon and I enjoy what I eat and what I drink and also just as much the moment when I become free of both and give back again to the earth what has been taken from her. Forgive this rude natural language..." (Alexander 1966:59n.1). Defecation is as pleasurable as eating. Eating and food are frequently perceived in terms of consequences.[1]

The ephemeral nature of food, as of life itself, proves to be a popular subject of German bathroom wall writings. In a latrinalia verse recorded in Wetti Himmlisch's putative Toilettenfrau's memoirs, we find a typical example (Himmlisch 1907:36):

Die grössten Meisterwerke der Küche	The greatest masterpieces of the kitchen
Geben hier die übelsten Gerüche.	Produce here the worst odors.
Je mehr die Köche zeigten ihre Künste,	The more the cooks practiced their skills
Je ärger hier duften die Abfuhrdünste.	The more awfully "sweet" the shit smells.
Da hilft nicht Ästhetik und nicht Devotion	Therefore neither care nor aesthetics will help
Hier bist du ein einfacher Erdensohn.	For here you are a simple down-to-earth person.

A more concise latrinalia couplet articulates the same equation as follows (Waldheim 1909:436): "Was für das Maul die Speise, ist für den Arsch die Scheisse." [What is food for the mouth is shit for the ass.] Still other verses pretend to give thanks that the process is not reversed, that is, that feces are eaten (Waldheim, 1910:404; Polsterer 1908:163; cf. Schenk 1912:503):

Hier ist der Ort, wo man ausscheisst, was man Tags zuvor gespeist; gottlob, dass wir nicht speisen müssen, was wir Tags zuvor geschissen.

Here is the place where one shits what one has eaten the day before. Praise God that we do not have to eat what we shit the day before.

In Germany, one can find material objects reflecting the German fascination with the transformation of food into feces. As was remarked by Freud, the figure of the Dukatenscheisser is a popular one, but it is even more striking that the figure should be available in confectionary shops in chocolate or marzipan, or other candy form. It is not clear how many cultures would relish the idea of eating a little figure who was depicted in the act of defecation. What these objects provide in part is a symbolic means of eating feces. This also explains the petite plastic mustard pots in the shape of toilet bowls, as well as the popularity of a shortbread biscuit (with rosewater as the distinguishing ingredient) called "Nonnenfürzchen" [nun's farts] (Spalding 1966:887). In terms of the anal erotic tendency to indulge in reversals, we have feces becoming food instead of the usual food becoming feces.

In view of the linkage between food and feces, it should not come altogether as a surprise to discover that certain specific foods are singled out in German folklore for their actual or imagined similarity to body waste products. Chocolate is one obvious example (cf. Legman 1975:924), as numerous allusions in folklore attest. For example, in a folksong version (Schweigmann 1970:129) of the folktale known to many by Chaucer's retelling of it in his celebrated Miller's Tale (Aarne-Thompson tale type 1361, The Flood), a peasant's blind son approaches the door of his beloved Grete:

Doch Grete hält nur den Arsch hinaus	Then Grete stuck only her ass out.
Und Hans, der gab ihr einen Kuss darauf.	And Hans gave her a kiss on it.
"Ach Grete, hast du ein breites Gesicht,	"Oh, Grete, have you a wide face
Du hast ja gar keine Neese nicht.	And you have no nose.

Ach Grete, Grete, du bist mein Leben	Oh Grete, Grete, you are my life
Doch hast du Schokolade um's Maul zu kleben."	Yet you have chocolate stuck around your mouth."

This tale is a popular one in Germany. A version of it appears in "The Serenade" episode of Wittenwiler's fifteenth-century *Ring* (Wittenwiler 1956:18). (Incidentally, bawdy as Chaucer's version is—the 'face' lets fly a fart—there is no mention there of "chocolate" around the "mouth.")

Another instance of chocolate usage was reported in 1908 from a seventy-year-old woman "aus gut bürgerlichen Kreisen" [from good bourgeois circles] who was overheard to issue the following flip invitation: "Trink Schokolade aus meinem Hintern" [Drink chocolate out of my rear end] (Amrain 1908:184).

There are modern examples as well. A children's rhyme reported in West Berlin in 1960 (Borneman 1974:180):

Ich weiss ne Frau,	I know a woman
Trinkt nur Kakao,	who drinks only cocoa,
Scheisst Schokolade	shits chocolate
Auf ihre Wade	on the calf of her leg
Ist das nicht schade?	Isn't that a pity?

Perhaps it is only a coincidence that German and especially Swiss chocolate is world-famous for its high quality.

If it isn't the food's color which is reminiscent of feces, it may be its smell. This may be one reason why cheese occurs frequently in scatological contexts. (See entries under "Käse" in Borneman 1971, or the children's rhymes in Borneman 1974:130–131.) One cannot help but think of German cheeses with strong scents, such as Harzer.

Chocolate and cheese may be obvious enough, but if there is one item which is regarded as typical of the German cuisine, it would have to be the sausage. Schalk observes, "Most conspicuous are the perennial, spotlessly-clean meat shops, lined with dozens of sausages, not to mention the numerous sausage stands everywhere" (1971:6) (For earlier accounts of the great variety and omnipresence of German sausages, see Mayhew 1864 1:39–40.) Although a sausage can obviously have phallic symbolic significance, it is in fact made from animal innards and its outer cover is normally an animal's intestine.

The anal associations of sausages are not something new invented in the twentieth century. We can find evidence in the seventeenth century of such an association in the correspondence of Liselotte mentioned earlier. In a letter dated October 31, 1694, written to Elisabeth Charlotte by her aunt, the wife of the Elector of Hanover possibly in response to the letter Liselotte wrote her complaining about her problems in relieving herself at Fontainebleau we find the following passage: "If meat makes shit, it is also true that shit makes meat.... Isn't it so that on the most delicate tables shit is served in ragouts.... the blood puddings, the chitterlings, the sausages, are they not ragouts in shit sacks?" (Bourke 1891:32).

Similarly, Goethe in his playlet "Hanswursts Hochzeit" begins with a description of John-Sausage (Hanswurst) which includes (Goethe 1964:488):

Seine Lust, in den Weg zu scheissen, Hab nicht können aus der Wurzel reissen.	His joy in shitting on the path cannot be uprooted.
Indes er sich am Arsche reibt Und Wurstel immer Wurstel bleibt.	Still he rubs himself in the ass and little sausage always remains little sausage.

The folkloristic data is unambiguous. Consider the following riddle reported from Zwickau in 1908 (Luedecke 1912:504):

Die drei grössten Weltwunder?	The three greatest wonders of the world?
Der Schniepel steht und hat keine Beine, die Votze hat ein Loch und kann Wasser halten, der Arsch hat keine Zähne und beisst die grössten Würste ab.	The penis stands and has no legs; the vagina has a hole and can hold water; and the ass has no teeth and can bite off the biggest sausages.

Other riddles confirm the usage: "Wann wird eine Knackwurst ungeniessbar?" [When is a knockwurst not edible?] "Wenn man das 'n' herausnimmt." [When one takes the 'n' out of it—which would make the German word "Kackwurst" or shit-wurst.] (Krauss and Reiskel 1905:34). Latrinalia is equally explicit (Luedecke 1907:321; Schnabel 1910:402):

In diesem Hotel gibts warme Würste ohne Schell (Schale).	In this hotel you can get warm wursts without skins.
Hier öffnet jeder Arsch sein Thor Und die Wurste kommen hervor, Und der Schwanz in aller Ruh Hängt daheben und sieht zu.	Here every ass opens its door and the wursts come forth and the penis in all the quiet hangs nearby and watches.

This understanding of wurst is contemporary. Günter Grass, for example, in *The Tin Drum* (1962:202) speaks of the SA troopers leaving "brown sausages" in the shops they loot in an updated version of *grumus merdae* (cf. Friedman 1968:175). There are also numerous children's rhymes (Borneman 1974:138–141) as well as an older folksong entirely devoted to "wurst." (Storck 1895:388).

The functional equivalence of cheese and sausage to feces is also suggested by the identity of meaning of the following alternative expressions:

Das ist mir scheissegal	Das ist mir Käse	Das ist mir Wurst
It is shit equal to me	It is cheese to me	It is sausage to me

All three expressions mean "it's all the same to me." Other evidence from folk speech confirms the scatological significance of chocolate and sausage—e.g., slang terms for the Toilettenfrau include "Schokoladenfrau" and "Würstchenfrau" (Borneman 1971:72.23).

We can now more fully appreciate why the Germans should enjoy eating sausages so much (and why they should choose to name one of their favorite folk characters Hanswurst). The fact that there are both sexual (phallic) and anal erotic associations for the same symbol 'wurst' is no obstacle in German culture.

The German love of sausages was evidently shared by German Jews. German Jews are Germans as well as being Jews. So we can now understand the reluctance of Polish Jews to eat German Jewish food. According to one source, the Polish Jews who settled in the Rhineland area became suspicious that the dishes used by the Jews of Germany did not meet the standards of ritual fitness. Polish Jews were told not to eat from the dishes of the German Jews because the Rhinelanders eat the scrapings of intestines and fats. A footnote explains that by fat was meant intestines and the like (Pollack, 1971:109–110, 282, n.108). Germans as well as German Jews had no problem in eating stuffed intestines in the form of sausages.

There are other German taste preferences that we can now better appreciate. For example, the Germans love wind instruments—especially brass—as is evident from the oom-pah-pah of German beer garden bands to the sophisticated use of horns in the music of Beethoven and Wagner. A traditional formula uttered after someone passes wind (cf. Rühmkorf, 1967:56) is:

Figure 10. A revealing postcard shows a "wind orchestra." (Reprinted from *Fantasy Postcards* copyright© 1975 by William Ouellette. All rights reserved. Reprinted by permission of Doubleday and Company, Inc. and William Ouellette)

Osso sagt Goethe, der Oss ist kein Flöte	Thus spake Goethe, the ass is no flute
Osso sagt Schiller, ein Proll ist kein Trille.	Thus spake Schiller, a fart is no trill.

A revealing German postcard from circa 1907 (Ouellette 1975:81) shows a scene of a "Wind Orchestra" in which a conductor in the center directs four wind instrument players (the instruments include a flute, trumpet and horn). (See figure 10.) The faces of all the players are buttocks and the sounds emitted from the instruments are clearly depicted as emanating from the anuses. A couplet (Limbach 1980:[44]) circulating among orchestra musicians confirms the metaphor. Was selbst Mozart anerkennt: der Hintern ist ein Instrument [What Mozart himself acknowledged: the backside is an instrument]. In this connection we may note that it has been suggested (Brophy 1964:254) that Mozart used "the explosion of air from brass instruments in a comic sense unmistakably parallel to his comic letters." The association between flatulence and music-making has been suggested by a number of writers (Merrill 1951:560; Collofino 1939:444–445) though without reference to Germany.

Another element of German culture which makes sense in the light of German anal eroticism is the delight in bathing in mud. Sometimes the German health resorts depend upon the alleged healing powers of mineral waters, but very often it is through the application of mud that the water's supposed remedial effect is achieved. If one stops to think about it, the very notion of a mud *bath* would seem to be a paradox, yet one need only scan a map of Germany to see the number of towns and villages whose names include an initial "bad" [bath], e.g., Baden-Baden, Wiesbaden, etc. Schalk in *The Germans* says (1971:52) "The discovery of a new mineral spring or the unearthing of a particularly fine mud variety is the German equivalent of striking oil in Texas. If the water or the mud can be medically proved as having healing qualities, the prefix "Bad" is triumphantly adopted and the community is in business."

It has also been observed that therapeutic bathing is widespread in Germany both in standard medical practice and in home treatment of minor complaints. According to Spindler (1973:62–63), German bath typology includes the "Sitzbad" (a simple tub bath in which one sits), the "Luftlichtbad" (the body is sprinkled with water after which the bather runs around naked breathing deeply), the "Dampfbad" (steam from boiling hay blossoms, oats, straw, or zinnia is directed to the afflicted body part which is covered with a saturated cloth to hinder evaporation), the "Bettdampfbad" (the naked patient is wrapped in a sheet previously placed in lukewarm water after which he is covered with wool blankets, and hot water bottles are put on the armpits and feet. After one or two hours of sweating, the patient is washed with cool water), the "Reibe-bad" (the patient sits on a small bench in a tub and rubs his body vigorously from the pit of the stomach down, with a towel dipped into cold water, the "Ganzwaschung" (the patient washes his entire body beginning with the feet and proceeding to the upper body and ending with the back), and, of course, the mud bath which is the same as the Sitzbad but with silt mixed in with the water.

From our previous discussion, we can see how the idea of bathing in mud fits into the "clean-dirty" paradigm. One bathes to get clean, but one bathes in mud to indulge in "dirt." Also relevant here is the erotic significance of mud in German culture. According to one source (Schalk 1971:324), in the red light district of Hamburg, one of the shows consists of nude girls wrestling in a ring of mud. The spectators close to the ring are protected with plastic caps. Thus the audience can remain clean while enjoying dirt!

Still another facet of German culture which may possibly be related to German national character is the development of printing. Every schoolboy is taught that the printing press was invented in fifteenth-century Germany and that Johann Gutenberg's Bible was the first printed book. One interesting piece of evidence supporting the contention that printing (*drucken*) may be associated with feces (*dreck*) is an initiation ritual reported among printers in the late nineteenth-century. (While philologists may argue that the words "drucken" and "dreck" are historically unrelated, this in no way prevents the folk from indulging in word play or otherwise associating the two terms.)

In April 1883, Philipp Scheidemann (1865-1939), who was later to become the first chancellor of the Weimar Republic, completed four years training as a printer's apprentice. The diploma, printed in five colors, proclaimed in rhyme:

> Purpur, Gold, Blau, Silber der Kaiser uns gab —
> Und schwarz drucken stets unser Lettern sich ab —
> Frei ist die Kunst!

> Purple, gold, blue, and silver, the Kaiser gave us —
> And our type (letters) are always printed in black.
> Long live the art!

But before the diploma was awarded, the apprentice had to undergo a form of baptism. However, the "holy water is not sprinkled on the head." Rather it is contained in a huge sponge placed on top of a proofreader's three-foot-high desk. "One is plumped down three times with considerable force on this sponge" while a strange incantation is muttered by the initiators:

> Pakkt an! Lasst seinen Corpus posteriorum fallen
> Auf diesen nassen Schwamm, bis triefen beide Ballen.
> Der durstigen Seele gebt ein Sturzbad oben drauff!
> Das ist dem Sohne Gutenbergs die allerbeste Tauff.

> Seize him! Let his rear end fall
> on this wet sponge til both balls are dripping wet.
> Give the thirsty soul a plunge-bath fresh and clean.
> That is the very best Christening of a son of Gutenberg.

The apprentice, having survived this ordeal, was then given a certificate of baptism attesting to the fact that Herr Philipp Scheidemann had undergone baptism by water *ad posteriora* and that he was duly admitted to the Black Art fraternity

(Schneidemann 1928:17-19; Lowie mentions the custom en passant though without commenting on its possible anal erotic significance, noting that an updated version of the practice occurred in 1948 [1954:122].)

At the very least, the emphasis upon cleaning the buttocks as part of an initiation ritual suggests the importance of infant care, but the specific association of printing letters in black followed by having one's rear end plunked down forcibly on a sponge does suggest an anal association for printing. The ritual *reversal* in the initiation is obvious enough. It is not the head which receives holy water, but the rear end. It is not the sponge which is applied to clean the buttocks, but the buttocks which are seemingly applied to the sponge.

This custom all by itself would hardly suffice to make a case for the anal erotic connections to printing, but once again the folklore data are helpful. A riddle provides a clue (Müller 1911:398):

> Welcher Unterschied ist zwischen einem Hund und einem Buch-
> drucker?
> What is the difference between a dog and a printer?

> Der Buchdrucker setzt erst und druckt dann, der Hund drückt erst
> und setzt dann.
> The printer first (type) sets and then prints; the dog strains first and
> then sets [his excrement].

The riddle surely suggests a printing-defecating equation. An alternative answer to the same riddle (Krauss and Reiskel 1905:45) provides another anal aspect:

> Leckt man den Hund im Arsch, so muss man seinen Schweif
> aufheben,
> was bei einem Buchdrucker nicht der Fall ist.

117

If one licks a dog in the ass, one must lift its tail
whereas with a printer, that is not the case.

A latrinalia verse collected in a private lodging house in the summer of 1910 makes the scatological usage of 'drücken' more explicit (Schnabel 1911:409):

Die Klappe auf	Open the lid,
Das Fenster zu	Close the window,
Setz dich mit deinem Nacktarsch drauf	Sit on it with your naked ass,
	And then push hard.
Und drücke dann feste zu.	

A more elaborate latrinalia verse (Polsterer 1908:164) confirms the equation:

Hier in diesem kleinen Reich	Here in this small state
Ist Hoch und Nieder gleich	High and low are equal
Ein jeder lässt hinab die Hose	Each one lets down his pants
Und die Keusche wie die Lose	The moral as well as the lax
Muss, will sie ihren Zweck erfüllen,	must, in order to fulfull this purpose,
Selbst das Heiligste enthüllen.	reveal even the most sacred part.
Freiheit herrscht im vollen Masse,	Freedom rules in full measure
Kein Zensor stecket seine Nase	No censor sticks his nose
In die Arbeit und dabei	in the works and thereby
Ist Satz, Druck und Presse frei.	printing, publishing, and the press are free.

The association of printing with defecation may help explain a curious fact in the history of medicine. One answer to the question "What is the earliest printed medical book?" is the Gutenberg *Laxierkalender* of 1457. Even though it consisted of only a single sheet of paper, it is interesting that the very first thing Gutenberg thought of printing after the Bible was a "Purgation-Calendar" indicating the best times and dates for

118

the utilization of laxatives. This isolated detail taken by itself might be thought insignificant, but in the context of the overall pattern of German national character delineated here, it seems totally consistent. (Cf. Krotus 1970:86).

Karl Abraham in his valuable essay on anal character did not single out printing, but he did remark that "the pleasure in looking at one's own mental creations, letters, manuscripts, etc. or completed works of all kinds has a prototype in the practice of looking at one's own feces" (1953:385). We have already seen how Mozart tended to equate writing with defecating. The interest in inspecting one's stool (or the stools of others) as a gauge of health might carry over into writing. According to Schalk (1971:60), in Germany, when someone applies for a job, he is commonly asked to write his curriculum vitae entirely in longhand. "This latter is usually analyzed for character traits by a graphologist." This sounds suspiciously analogous to diagnostics through stool analysis.

As my last attempt to demonstrate the utility of the type of analysis undertaken in this essay, I should like to examine selected aspects of anti-Semitism in Germany. While it would be foolish to think that the anal eroticism of Germans could explain the ultimate causes of so complex a phenomenon, I do think it can illuminate some of the practices of it in Germany. It is, of course, not that uncommon for minority groups to be referred to as "dirty" by the majority group members among whom they live. Still, as I shall document, the image of the Jew in Germany is very closely tied to feces.

A longstanding ethnic-slur tradition in Germany depicts Jews as suckling from a pig. (See figure 11.) This so-called "Judensau" [Jew-sow] can be traced in graphics going back at least to the fourteenth century. Joshua Trachtenberg in his book *The Devil*

Figure 11. This so-called "Judensau" can be traced in graphics going back at least to the fourteenth century. (Courtesy of the Warburg Institute, University of London.)

and the Jews observes that "the notorious figure of the *Juden-sau* portraying the sow as the mother feeding her Jewish off-spring" was one of the commonest caricatures of the Jew in the middle ages (1966:26; cf. Fuchs 1921:114-116 and Kaufmann 1890).

In a comprehensive and profusely illustrated monograph devoted to the Judensau, Isaiah Shachar traces the image through more than six hundred years, from the thirteenth-century to the sixteenth-century in German architectural sculpture and from the fifteenth to the nineteenth-century in various graphic arts. According to Shachar, "It was carved on corbels and choir stalls in several cathedrals and churches, and on buttresses and gutter spouts of others. It appeared on gates, on public and private buildings, and became the subject of a wall painting in the passage of a Frankfurt bridge-tower as well as of later paintings." Shachar specifically remarks that "From its earliest occurrences, the "Judensau" was *confined to German-speaking territories,* within which it spread widely and from which it rarely found its way abroad" (1974:1, my emphasis). The Judensau image is particularly strange in the light of the traditional Jewish antipathy to eating pork. But the iconographic ethnic slur is crystal clear.

Sometimes the Judensau is shown eating feces. In a tract entitled "Against Hanswurst" written in 1541, Luther speaks to his readers in this fashion: "But think what you will, so dirty your pants, hang it round your neck, then make a jelly of it and eat it like the vulgar sows and asses you are" (1966:187). Pigs do eat feces and it is precisely their propensity to do so that explains why *schwein* is such an offensive insult in German folk speech. The implication is that the object of the insult is a shit-eater. In this sense, a swine is equivalent to the LMIA insult.

Dogs too are thought to eat feces (cf. Collofino 1939:193) and furthermore their characteristic sniffing behavior involving a rival dog's posterior is almost certainly perceived by Germans to be an animal version of LMIA. Thomas Mann in his 1918 novel *A Man and his Dog* describes the typical encounter of a dog with a stranger: "So he walks up to the spot and, with a humble and inscrutable mien, fulfils that act of sacrifice which, as he well knows, always brings about a certain pacification and temporary reconciliation with the other dog—so long as he too performs the same act" (Mann 1930:83; for a discussion of the scatological allusions in this novel, see Rollfinke 1977:119-133).

Additional evidence supporting the contention that the Germans are inclined to perceive canine greeting custom in this fashion is provided by a common children's toy "Magnetische Hunde" [Magnetic Dogs]. Instructions for the toy read: "Place the dogs on a polished surface and lean one dog against the other, head to head or from the side, and withdraw quickly." Once released, the magnets force the two dogs into the standard LMIA position. The possible oicotypical significance of the German version of this toy is suggested by a comparison with the American version in which the magnets force the dogs into a nose-to-nose encounter. (See figure 12).

This is no doubt why the combination of pig and dog is doubly powerful: *Schweinehund!* The epithet is analogous to such doubling as *Scheissdreck*. Both pigs and dogs are thought by Germans to eat feces. Incidentally, the public use of the pig-dog epithet was, according to laws current in Saxony in 1862, subject to fine. For a person to call another a "swinehound cost 7 s. and 34 d., while there were reduced rates for lesser offenses. For example, to call another person a 'schwein-

Figure 12. German magnetic dogs (left) compared with the American version (right). (Photo by Gene Prince).

hundchen' (or little dog of the same breed) was only 5 s. and 6 d." (Mayhew 1864 2:649).

But to return to the Judensau image, let us be sure we understand the linkage. Pigs eat shit and Jews suckle from pigs. Hence Jews indirectly nurse from feces. Sometimes the imagery is even more direct. While a few Jews suckle, others are depicted as kneeling behind the mother sow and eating the sow's feces (Feldhaus 1921:94; Fuchs 1921:31; Trachtenberg 1966:8). A sixteenth-century woodcut shows just such a scene. A textual caption makes the action explicit: "Saug du die Milch, Friss du den Dreck, Das ist doch euer best Geschleck" [Suck thou the milk, Eat thou the dirt. Is this not your favorite delicacy?] (Fuchs 1921:126).

The image of the Jews as dirty eaters of pig feces is also featured in Martin Luther's virulent anti-Semitic tract entitled "On the Jews and Their Lies," first published in 1543. At one point, speaking directly to Jews, Luther says, "You are not worthy of looking at the outside of the Bible, much less of reading it. You should read only the bible that is found under the sow's tail, and eat and drink the letters that drop there" (Luther 1971:212) (The idea of defecating alphabetical letters is still in oral tradition, for example, "rede oder kack Buchstaben" [speak or shit letters] which constitutes a rude exhortation to someone to say something, anything, no matter what (Spalding 1958:419). The quotation from Luther, by the way, is another piece of evidence for the printing-defecating equation discussed earlier.) Luther's equating Jews with feces is made on a number of occasions. In his *Table Talk,* we find the following (1911:289):

> When we read that Judas hanged himself, that his belly burst in pieces, and that his bowels fell out, we may take this as a sample how it will go with all Christ's enemies. The Jews ought to have made a mirror of Judas, and have seen therein how they in like manner should be destroyed. An allegory or mystery herein lies hid, for the belly signifies the whole kingdom of the Jews, which shall also fall away and be destroyed, so that nothing there of shall remain. When we read that the bowels fell out, this shows the posterity of the Jews, their whole generation, shall be spoiled and go to the ground.

Luther was quite serious. His solution to the Jewish problem—he referred to the Jews as "a heavy burden, a plague, a pestilence, a sheer misfortune for our country" (1971:265, 275) — was straightforward enough. "If we wish to wash our hands [note the metaphor] of the Jews' blasphemy," he said, "and not share in their guilt, we have to part company with them. They must be driven from our country." Rulers who had Jewish subjects "must act like a good physician who, when gangrene has set in, proceeds without mercy to cut, saw, and burn flesh, veins, bone, and marrow" (1971:288, 292). Luther went so far as to recommend a number of specific points of action to be taken (1971:268-272; cf. 285-286):

> "First, to set fire to their synagogues or schools and to bury and cover with dirt whatever will not burn, so that no man will ever

124

again see a stone or cinder of them...Second, I advise that their houses also be razed and destroyed...Third, I advise that all their prayer books and Talmudic writings, in which such idolatry, lies, cursing, and blasphemy are taught, be taken from them...Fourth, I advise that their rabbis be forbidden to teach henceforth on pain of loss of life and limb...Fifth, I advise that safe-conduct on the highways be abolished completely for Jews...

Sixth, I advise that usury be prohibited to them, and that all cash and treasure of silver and gold be taken from them and put aside for safekeeping...Seventh, I recommend putting a flail, an ax, a hoe, a spade, a distaff, or a spindle into the hands of young, strong Jews and Jewesses and letting them earn their bread in the sweat of their brow..."

There in 1543, one can see the seeds of Kristallnacht in 1938, when 119 synagogues in all parts of Germany along with many Jewish homes and shops were burned to the ground. Even the philosophy of labor concentration camps is articulated by Luther, though encampment per se is not mentioned.

Luther's reference to usury reminds us of the regulations forbidding usury to all but Jews. But the money-feces symbolism so common in Germany no doubt served to confirm the Jews' involvement with dirt and filth. An anti-Semitic caricature of the early nineteenth-century shows a Jewish baby shitting money into a pot surrounded by admiring Jews (Fuchs, 1921:104). The additional association in Germany of the Jews with the devil was yet another link in the chain of events which led to the depiction of the Jews as feces. (Recall Luther's depiction of the devil in anal terms.)

There were other contributing factors. (Pollack 1971:1) observes that in some instances Jews were forced to live in less desirable sections of cities. "Thus, the Portuguese Jews of Hamburg lived close to the 'debris mound,' dreckwall, the city refuse dump...the Frankfort Jews had their homes 'near the moat' of the city which was used for 'garbage disposal.'" Such physical geography obviously confirmed the association of Jews with dirt.

If Jews were dirty, then they were a threat to cleanliness. A proverb proclaims "Wer sein Haus rein halten will, der verschliess die Tür vor Juden und Huren" [Whoever wants to keep his house clean should shut his door to Jews and whores] (Fuchs 1921:198). One of the favorite Nazi charges against oppositional elements, not just Jews, was that they "soil" the purity of the fatherland (Kecskemeti and Leites 1948:257). There is good reason to believe that the linkage of Jews with dirt culminated in the ideology of Nazi Germany, one goal of which was *Judenreinmachen:* to make Germany clean of Jews. The very word *Judenrein* clearly implies the existence of the basic premise—that Jews are dirty. The fanatic concern with racial purity is in part a logical extension of the reaction formation from severe infantile toilet training. Transforming such a racial fantasy into grim reality led to the holocaust. The symbolic proof of this notion comes from the specifics the Nazis employed in the deathcamps. Jews were taken into showers—why showers? Gas could have been introduced by a number of other means. The symbology in the light of the German national character profile delineated here suggests that the intent was to clean up Germany—by eliminating the Jews. The use of ovens smacked of garbage disposal.

One should also remember that sometimes the liquidation of Jews was quite literal. For example, in the Danzig Anatomic Institute during the years 1943 and 1944, experiments in the production of soap from human fat were carried out. After corpses, naked and headless, arrived at the Institute, they were stored in metal containers containing a preservative mixture for approximately four months, the mixture facilitating the separation of tissue from bones. The tissue was then boiled for several days. According to testimony (International Military Tribunal 1947:597-599) presented at Nuremberg in February 1946 by one of the direct participants in these experiments, a laboratory assistant at the Institute, it took 70 to 80 kilograms of human fat collected from some 40 bodies to yield 25 kilograms of soap. Such bars of soap "made from pure Jewish fat" were proudly distributed to German soldiers. Digits on the soap indicated the number of the extermination camp. In terms of the present investigation, we seem to have here a mad metaphorical *reduction ad absurdum* in which, through a fiendish triumph of technology, "dirty" Jewish flesh was melted down in order to transform it into "clean" soap.

There is no need to recapitulate in detail all the unspeakable horrors of Auschwitz and the other death camps, but the various heart-rendering accounts of survivors amply document the distinct anal component of life in those hell-holes. Terrence Des Pres in his book *The Survivor: An Anatomy of Life in the Death Camps,* first published in 1976, presents a gruesome composite picture based on a survey of dozens of eyewitness accounts. His third chapter, "Excremental Assault," gives shocking details of how the inmates were subjected to constant humiliation and degradation through anal means. Although signs were posted at Auschwitz and elsewhere demanding cleanliness—typical notices were "There's only one road to freedom. Its milestones are: Cleanliness, Punctuality, Obedience..." "Be clean," "Keep this place clean and tidy" (Kraus and Kulka 1966:35, 45, 126), the camp overseers made it absolutely impossible to be clean.

> There was one latrine for thirty to thirty-two thousand women and we were permitted to use it only at certain hours of the day. We stood in line to get into this tiny building, knee-deep in human

excrement. As we all suffered from dysentery, we could rarely wait until our turn came, and soiled our ragged clothes, which never came off our bodies, thus adding to the horror of our existence by the terrible smell which surrounded us like a cloud. The latrine consisted of a deep ditch with planks thrown across it at certain intervals. We squatted on these planks like birds perched on a telegraph wire, so close together that we could not help soiling one another (Des Pres 1977:58).

This report is typical and is echoed over and over again in other accounts. "Those with dysentery melted down like candles, relieving themselves in their clothes, and swiftly turning into stinking repulsive skeletons who died in their own excrement." "Some of the patients died before they ever reached the gas chambers. Many of them were covered all over with excrement, for there were no sanitary facilities, and they could not keep themselves clean." (Des Pres 1977:59).

The lack of adequate facilities was exacerbated by the lack of toilet paper: "there was no paper in the whole of Auschwitz...and I would have to 'find another way out.' I tore off a piece of my scarf and washed it after use. I retained this little piece throughout my days in Auschwitz; others did likewise" (Des Pres 1977:59).

One poignant account of the Sachsenhausen camp, recalls the plight of a very sick 75-year-old professor from the University of Warsaw. Suffering from severe dysentery, the professor begged to be carried into the toilet room and left there to sleep. One night the author discovered the professor lying in the toilet room, "his face was smeared with excrement," his hands covered with slime. In a whispered voice, the professor asked "Could you lend me a little piece of newspaper? I will give you twice as much tomorrow." By chance, the author possessed a whole newspaper (which he had obtained in exchange for half of his bread ration) and handed it to the professor. The professor tore off the first page of the newpaper and held out the rest to the author. "Thank you very much," he gasped and tears ran down his face. The author said, "No, it is all for you," and did not take back the paper. The old man was deeply grateful. "Is it really all for me?...I am so very happy. This is something I will never forget. How much suffering it will save me! I cannot tell you how glad I am now." The author comments, "An old dirty newspaper had become the supreme blessing of a man who a few months before had been the pride of Polish scholarship, honored wherever learning is prized" (Szalet 1945:157-158, 211-213). Something as simple as toilet paper cannot be appreciated until it is totally absent.

During the night when it was forbidden or dangerous to use the latrines, inmates with diarrhea were forced to use their soup bowls or pans for coffee. Then they hid the utensils under the mattress to avoid the punishment for doing this (twenty-five strokes on the bare buttocks, or kneeling all night long on sharp gravel, holding up bricks). These punishments (for defecating in one's eating utensil) often ended in the death of the "guilty" (Des Pres 1977:60). The forced use of eating utensils as toilet articles was a ghastly literalization of the metaphor of making an enemy eat shit. A number of incidents demonstrate this metaphor: "After the men had just started to eat, an overseer suddenly announced that the time was up for the roll call. He made the prisoners pour their soup into the toilets, so that the majority went hungry" (Bluhm 1948:19-20). On another occasion, the men "were ordered to drink out of the toilet bowls. The men could not bring themselves to obey; they only pretended to. But the 'block leaders forced their heads deep into the bowls until they were covered with excrement. At that they almost went out of their minds—that was why their screams had sounded so demented'" (Bluhm 1948:16). "In Birkenau, soup bowls were periodically taken from the prisoners and thrown into the latrine, from which they had to be retrieved: 'When you put it to your lips for the first time, you smell nothing suspicious. Other pairs of hands trembling with impatience wait for it, they seize it the moment you have finished drinking. Only later, much later, does a repelling odor hit your nostrils'" (Des Pres 1977:63). These and other accounts show how the Auschwitz routine compelled inmates to eat feces.

"The first days our stomachs rose up at the thought of using what were actually chamber pots at night. But hunger drives, and we were so starved that we were ready to eat any food. That it had to be handled in such bowls could not be helped. During the night, many of us availed ourselves of the bowls secretly. We were allowed to go to the latrines only twice each day. How could we help it? No matter how great our need, if we went out in the middle of the night we risked being caught by the S.S., who had orders to shoot first and ask questions later" (Des Pres 1977:64).

It has been suggested that these techniques were employed to reduce the adult inmates to the level of totally dependent infants who were in a pre-toilet training state. It is noteworthy that according to one report the most commonly stated motives given in Germany for child abuse were concerned with cleanliness training, and in several instances, parents angry about their infants soiling themselves actually forced these infants to put their faces into the excrement and ordered them to eat it (Ende 1979-1980:259-260). In the camps, in effect, the overseers were strict parents who had the power to prevent children from using the bathrooms. "The favorite pastime of one Kapo was to stop prisoners just before they reached the latrine. He would force an inmate to stand at attention for questioning; then make him 'squat in deep knee-bends until the poor man could no longer control his sphincter and 'exploded'"; then beat him; and only then, "covered with his own excrement, the victim would be allowed to drag himself to the latrine" (Des Pres 1977: 62-63). One writer tells of the chill that went down his spine during a visit to Austria in 1968 when a middle-aged Austrian farmer showed him with pride his scrapbook of World War II. He boasted about a picture showing him in SS uniform hovering over an aged Jewish rabbi forced to clean an outhouse (Schalk 1971:138).

The writers about Auschwitz and other camps have given us an unforgettable picture of the unspeakable tortures of everyday life, and Des Pres is quite right when he observes "The fact is that prisoners were *systematically* subjected to filth. They were the deliberate target of excremental assault" (1977:63). But I do not believe he or other students of the holocaust have realized the connection between these incredible acts of brutality and the trait of German national character I have been at some pains to describe. The death camps were, from this perspective, just one more illustration of the critical distinction between those who shit on and those who are shit upon. Power belongs to the shitters; powerlessness is the fate of the victims of the shitters.

An unusual daydream reported by Jung suggests the anal nature of aggression. "I found my thoughts returning again to the beautiful cathedral which I loved so much, and to God sitting on the throne—and then my thoughts would fly off again

131

as if they had received a powerful electric shock." Jung is unable to complete the thought or tell his mother what is bothering him. Finally on the third night

> "I awoke from a restless sleep just in time to catch myself thinking again about the cathedral and God. I had almost continued the thought! I felt my resistance weakening. Sweating with fear, I sat up in my bed to shake off sleep. Now it is coming, now it's serious! *I must think….I gathered all my courage, as though I were about to leap forthwith into hell-fire, and let the thought come. I saw before me the cathedral, the blue sky. God sits on His golden throne, high above the world—and from under the throne an enormous turd falls upon the sparkling new roof, shatters it, and breaks the walls of the cathedral asunder…So that was it! I felt an enormous, an indescribable relief. (Jung 1973:36-40).*

Here, although Jung certainly doesn't analyze his dream in this way, is an example of an authority figure using the power of his anus to destroy.

A German postcard from World War I provides another illustration of the anal nature of aggression. A large woman is lying face down on the ground not far from Bucharest. Her buttocks are on top of a wheel axle and from them are issuing forth projectiles falling on the city. The postcard bears the caption *But Bertha,* referring to "Big Bertha" the familiar name for the 420 mm gun employed during the war (Holt 1977:64).

One of the most common latrinalia verses confirms the symbolic linkage between artillery and anal activity. The following text was reported in Silesia in 1894 (Luedecke 1907:323; for other versions, see Gerhardt 1908:270; Thorner 1909:437-438; Ihm 1912:498; Ruhmkorf 1967:43-44; Borneman 1974:54):

132

Was ist der Mensch? Ein Erdenkloss,	What is man? A clod of earth
gefärbt [often gefüllt] mit roter Tinte;	colored (filled) with red ink
das Loch ist wie ein Taler gross	The hole is large as a Taler
und vorne hängt die Flinte.	And in front hangs the musket.
Und drunter hängt der Pulversack,	and under it hangs the powdersack
gefüllt mit zwei Patronen,	filled with two cartridges,
und hinten ist der Schiesseplatz,	and behind is the shooting place
da donnern die Kanonen.	And from there thunder the cannons.

There is a reason, I think, why this particular piece of folk poetry is so widespread in Germany. The reason may be that it so succinctly encapsulates a portion of German worldview. Man is viewed as a military instrument with the phallus as gun and the anus as cannon. We know that the German's self-stereotype has long included a glorification of military prowess (Dundes 1975:37). What is of special interest here is the explicit labelling of the anus as a weapon of bombardment.

The use of feces as a weapon to keep enemies at bay is also manifest in another latrinalia verse (cf. Krotus 1970:18):

Auf diesem Scheisshaus sitzt ein Geist,	On this shithouse sits a ghost
der dem andern in den Hintern beisst.	who bites the posterior of the other [who sits there]
Doch hat er mich noch nicht gebissen,	But he has not yet bitten me
Denn hab ich ihm auf den Kopf geschissen.	For I have shit on his head.

Another folk poem (Anon. 1968:41) recommends a similar course of action:

Bestrafte Hinterlist	Punished trick
Wenn einer wusst, wie einem ist,	If a person would like to know how it is
Wenn einer sitzt und scheisst,	if one sits and shits,
Und einer ihm voll Hinterlist	and someone full of trickery
In seine Eier beisst.	bites his balls.
Das Beste ist in diesem Fall:	The best (thing) to do in this case:
Man kehrt sich daran nicht,	One pays no attention to it,
Man kauft sich einen Löwenmut	One buys a (portion of) lion's courage
Und scheisst ihm in's Gesicht.	And shits into his face.

It is quite likely that the German interest and expertise in bombing was partly inspired by the anal nature of aggression. Airplanes releasing bombs from their bowels so to speak would be metaphorically appropriate (cf. Markowitz 1969:101, Sabbath and Hall 1977:209). In any event, regardless of the possible anal significance of aerial bombardment—and what of the development of such "gas" inflated flights of fancy as dirigibles and zeppelins?—we can see the consistent pattern in German history of having enemies and victims on the receiving end of an anal attack. It is in this psychological context that the brutal life in the death camps must be seen.

Richard L. Rubenstein, in his book *After Auschwitz* does suggest an anal interpretation of the death camps—although without reference to a full-scale study of German national character (cf. Markowitz 1969:91). He claims that the Nazis themselves referred to Auschwitz as the "anus mundi" (1966:32). German medical doctors who served in the death camps were interviewed by Yale psychiatrist Robert Jay Lifton. One commented coldly that "life at Auschwitz was as routine as 'building a sewage project.'" (Anon 1979b:68). Such direct

134

quotes confirm the German perception of the Jews as dirt, as garbage, as sewage to be eliminated.

The symbolic equivalence of defecation and death may well be cross-cultural. In this standard analogy, the intake of food is associated with life while the end result, feces, is likened to a corpse. But however widespread this metaphorical equation may be, there can be no doubt of its overpowering presence in German culture. The philosopher Schopenhauer in *Die Welt Als Wille und Vorstellung* [The World as Will] gives us one articulation of it: "Constant nourishment and renewal differ from generation only in degree, and only in degree does constant excretion differ from death...the process of generation is a higher power of nourishment...On the other hand, excretion, the constant exhalation and throwing off of matter, is the same as what at a higher power is death." Schopenhauer goes so far as to say that the process of replenishment is part of life and that one should not lament the discarded matter. "It appears just as foolish to embalm corpses as it would be carefully to preserve our excreta," he writes (1958:277).

The point is stated simply that if the Germans have a preoccupation with defecation and feces, they may also have one with death and corpses. Günter Grass in his poem "Excrement rhymed" in *The Flounder* (1978:280) expresses this thought: "All poems that prophesy and rhyme on death are excrement that has dropped from a constipated body." Erich Fromm in his attempt to redefine Freudian anal character into what he terms necrophilia (1973:330, 366) in effect also confirms the equivalence of feces and death. In this respect we may mention a comparative analysis undertaken of a German and an American school song book. One of the findings was that "30 of the German songs (8.3 percent) lauded heroic death, while in the American medium there is no mention of death of any sort" (Sebald 1961:320). The implication here is also that just as Americans are more reluctant than the Germans to mention feces so they are also more reluctant to discuss death.

The question of the German attitude toward death could quite obviously be a whole separate study, but if feces and corpses are symbolic equivalents, and if Jews are also considered to be feces, then transforming Jews into corpses at death/sewage disposal facilities made metaphorical sense. Twisted and perverted as such an outrageous idea is, one must remember that such repugnant and inhumane acts did occur. Their documented occurrence is de facto evidence that the specifics of such genocide are not incompatible with German national character. This means that the death camps cannot be blamed solely on several peculiar individuals. We may briefly turn to consider Hitler in this connection.

Hitler's mother was reported to be "an exemplary housekeeper and there was never a spot or speck of dust to be found in the house" (Langer 1972:149,105). One psychiatrist surmises, "From what we know about his mother's excessive cleanliness and tidiness we may assume that she employed rather stringent measures during the toilet training period of her children." Writing his report during the war, the psychiatrist continues, "That a residual tension from this period still exists in Hitler is evidenced by the frequency of imagery in his speaking and writing that deals with dung and dirt and smell" (Langer 1972:163). Robert G. L. Waite in his 1977 book *The Psychopathic God Adolf Hitler* discusses Hitler's anal eroticism in some detail. "Hitler often talked about dirt. People he disliked were usually described as being filthy. Thus the schoolteachers who gave him unsatisfactory grades had *"filthy* necks and uncared for beards"; modern artists sat on the "*dung-heap* of literary Dadaism"; and liberals were "dirty and false."...The Jews were particularly filthy: "The smell of these caftan wearers often made me ill. Added to this were their dirty clothes..." "If the Jews were alone in this world they would suffocate...in *dirt* and *filth*." Hitler used the same kind of word in speaking of the Jewish people, "Entjudung" (de-Jewing), as one would use in speaking of delousing or fumigation. (1977:25). Fromm in his sketch of Hitler as "A clinical case of Necrophilia" (1973:369–433) claims that Hitler had a compulsive tendency towards overcleanliness (1973:405).

Another relevant quotation from Hitler is "And when he [the Jew] turns the treasures over in his hand they are transformed into dirt and dung" (Langer 1972:164). Thus Hitler suggests that the Jews have the Midas touch in reverse. (The Midas touch incidentally is very likely a symbolic rendering of the idea that everything one touches turns to shit. Remember that one of King Midas' problems was that he was unable to eat anything since all objects touched turned to gold.) (Cf. Aarne-Thompson tale type 775, Midas' Short-sighted Wish). If Jews turned treasures into dirt and dung, then the obvious solution was to turn Jews into dirt and dung.

Actually it was Hitler who was obsessed with the idea of his own body transforming food into feces. Reports attest to his fear that his body odors were offensive and he was so disturbed by his flatulence that he took huge quantities of "Dr. Koster's Anti-Gas Pills" which contained strychnine and atropin (Langer 1972:235). This is reminiscent of the conviction of Alfred Krupp (1812–1887), the founder of the armaments dynasty, that his own body odors were toxic (Manchester 1968:42,146). Interestingly enough, Krupp also believed the scent of horse manure to be inspiring and felt that he became creative in its presence, so much so that he designed his ideal mansion, Villa Hügel, in such a way that his study was directly over the stable complete with air shafts to allow the scents to rise up to him (Manchester 1968:42,110). A doctor once visiting Krupp's sickly son Fritz actually complained that the house smelled like a horse's latrine, and Krupp's wife Bertha bitterly resented his "fetishistic admiration for manure" (Manchester 1968:182, 194).

Hitler was sufficiently concerned about his body odors to alter his diet. He was convinced that eating vegetables improved the odors of his flatulence (Waite 1977:26). Waite tells us (1977:149) "He also worried a good deal about his feces and examined them often, as his doctors reported to U.S. intelligence officers after the war. To alleviate chronic constipation, he frequently took enemas, which he insisted upon administering himself."

The reference to constipation reminds us that Luther and Kant may also have suffered from constipation (Erikson 1958:176, 232; Stuckenberg 1882:98). (It is interesting that both Hitler and Kant tried to avoid perspiring [Hitler 1953:464; Stuckenberg 1882:161].) Twentieth-century German artist and political cartoonist George Grosz in trying to explain the Nazism of his countrymen suggested that Germans are "quick to catch the disease of anti-humanity," explaining, "I think it is, on the whole because of their poor elimination. Yes, I am sorry to say, I think Germany is a headquarters for constipation" (Hecht 1964:140–141). Whether constipation is really more common in Germany than elsewhere or whether constipation can be blamed for alleged national characteristics is open to question. What is significant here is that German intellectuals believe or at least say they believe that constipation is critical to German character. One thinks, for example, of Nietzsche's repeated assertions in *Beyond Good and Evil* and *Ecco Homo* that "German profundity is often merely a hard and sluggish 'digestion'" or that the origin of the German spirit is "from distressed intestines" (Kaufman 1968:396, 694, 696). In this connection, we may cite an older literary allusion "mein Eingeweide" [my intestines] which refers to one's innermost being (Spalding 1961:573). It is the specific choice of intestines to provide the metaphor for one's *heart*felt feelings that is of interest here.

One of Hitler's favorite anecdotes about himself concerned an incident during his schoolboy days and it was a story he repeatedly told on himself to his secretaries and his military associates. After his school examinations at Steyr, he recalled that for the only time in his life he got drunk. When he returned to his lodgings, his landlady asked him if he had obtained his certificate. Hitler searched through his pockets. "I turned them inside out. Not a trace of my certificate! What could I have done with it, and what was I to show my mother," he said according to the report in Hitler's *Table Talk*. He began to make up possible excuses such as a gust of wind carried it off from an open train window. Hitler's landlady suggested he return to the school to seek a duplicate of the document and she even loaned him the fare to do this. Then according to Hitler (1953:160), "The director began by keeping me waiting for quite a long time. My certificate had been brought back to the school, but torn into four pieces and in a somewhat inglorious condition. It appeared that, in absent-mindedness of intoxication, I had confused the precious parchment with toilet paper. I was overwhelmed. I cannot tell you what the

139

director said to me, I am still humiliated." Of course, inasmuch as Hitler kept on telling the humiliating story, this indicates that Hitler enjoyed reliving the experience and so the story is itself an indication of his anal fixation as psychiatrist Waite remarks (1977:149). (The incident also demonstrates Hitler's basic scorn for the values of education—he often made fun of "professors.")

Hitler's propensity for self-denigration is suggested by his referring to himself as a "Scheisskerl" [a shit churl or shithead] which was supposedly one of his favorite words (Waite 1977:149, 449n.53). Such self-deprecation or self-degradation would be entirely in accord with his alleged coprolagic behavior. He supposedly derived satisfaction from having a woman urinate or defecate on his face. While there is admittedly some dispute as to whether such activities did or did not occur—it was obviously extremely difficult to obtain reliable eyewitness accounts—there is considerable evidence to indicate that this coprophilic activity did in fact happen—with his niece Geli (Angela) Raubal. (Of the seven women who were sexually involved with Hitler, six committed suicide or seriously attempted to do so. One of these was Geli Raubal in 1931.) Waite concludes that Hitler did have this perversion (Waite 1977:243) and he believes that the high suicide rate among his paramours supports this widespread rumor (1977:239; cf. Langer 1972:171).

In judging the act, one should keep in mind the longstanding popularity of the LMIA gesture in German culture. But whether or not Hitler participated in sexual activities of this sort, there is plenty of other evidence of his anal fixation and his special fascination with feces and flatulence. One might even conjecture on the relevance of his initial occupational choice of

140

painting as perhaps being related to the infantile delight in smearing feces. There is folklore data to support the possible fecal underpinnings of painting. A children's rhyme reported from Frankfurt (Alderheiden 1929:235; cf. Borneman 1976a:99–100), one of several poking fun at occupations, runs:

| Maler und Lackierer | Painter and lacquerer |
| Beschisser und Beschmierer | (Be)shitter and (be)smearer |

With respect to the possible influences on Nazi ideology or esthetics of anal erotic factors, it is also tempting to speculate about brown as the preeminently favorite color for clothing and uniforms (cf. Bosmajian 1979).[2] But Hitler's possible or probable anal eroticism is not germane, although I would argue that it is German. (With respect to acts of coprophagia or coprolagnia, it might be noted that the majority of case histories cited by Havelock Ellis come from German sources, e.g., Kraft-Ebbing and Moll [Ellis 1920:63–69].) One individual's fantasy or nightmare cannot become a reality unless others in a culture are predisposed or willing to share it. Thus the idiosyncrasies of Adolf Hitler's personality are not the issue. What is of concern is that Adolf Hitler, like Germans centuries before him, saw the world through fecal lenses. As enemies were feces, the way to eliminate them was by means of an elaborate purge. The cultural association of Jews with feces did not begin with Hitler. The Judensau iconography goes back to well before Luther. Hitler and his compatriots simply used the Judensau for political purposes, hoping that by ritually killing millions of innocent scapegoats his power would be ensured.

As we approach the end of this essay, a few points ought to be kept in mind. The aim of the present investigation, I remind you, was to consider the overall question of whether or not the folklore of a given group reflects the character of that group. I believe the answer based upon the data presented is affirmative. German folklore (and for that matter German literature and culture generally) demonstrates a propensity for anal eroticism. I am not saying that the Germans are the only people on the face of the earth with an interest in scatology. One need only cite Rabelais in France or Jonathan Swift in England (cf. Pops 1982) or refer to such American classics on flatulence as Mark Twain's *1601* or Benjamin Franklin's proposal for the amelioration of flatal aromas through diet. The French, for example, would appear to have a predilection for flatulence but not so much for defecation. A good many of the treatises devoted to flatulence were written in French (Cf. Collofino 1939:106–108, 803, 813–814 and the *Bibliotheca Scatologica*). There is also the curious case of Joseph Pujol, Le Petomane, who gave musical performances of a kind on French stages at the turn of the century (Nohain and Caradec 1967; cf. Legman 1975:870–871). But the lightness of flatulence seems closer to French culture than the heaviness of feces in German culture, if one may risk indulging in stereotypes. So the issue is a matter of degree, not of kind. Anal character is certainly not limited to Germanic peoples, but I would argue that it is indeed found among Germanic peoples.

Ideally, in national character studies, one should show both that a nation has a specific trait and that other nations do not. So in that sense, it is not enough to prove beyond a reasonable doubt that the Germans have a preoccupation with feces. I should also have to demonstrate that other peoples do not share a similar concern. Unfortunately, to do this properly, I would have to carry out extensive research on a staggering variety of cultures—even if I confined myself to Europe. Does French, Italian, Spanish, Portuguese, Danish, Polish, Swedish, Czech, Russian, etc. folklore contain the same concentration of anal erotic elements as does German folklore? The difficulties of making a properly rigorous statistical search for the absence of a trait should be obvious enough.

One cannot always rely on the published record, especially when taboo subject matter is involved. It is in theory possible that many countries, e.g., in Europe, have the same quantities of anal idioms as do the Germans but that only the Germans have painstakingly bothered to record them from medieval times to the present. It would then be misleading to compare the richly documented German evidence with the unwritten, unrecorded traditions of other cultures. (The question would still remain, however, why the Germans were so industrious and meticulous in preserving their past materials.) I can only say for certain that from my knowledge of American folklore, there are far more scatological elements in German folklore. I might appropriately cite a brief study which compared the contents of German Frau Wirtin verses with their Anglo-American counterparts: the limerick. In that study, it is noted that these forms circulate among the educated segments of both societies. But whereas anal-excretory motifs appear in the Frau Wirtin verses enjoyed by the German-speaking intelligentsia, "No such prevalence of anal-excretory motifs is found in limericks circulating among English-speaking intelligentsia" (Wells 1951:94). It is an extremely difficult task to compare the metaphorical traditions of two different cultures. So often these traditions depend upon peculiarities of idiom which are literally incomparable. An American criticizing someone who was making a great to-do of a trivial matter might refer to "making a mountain out of a molehill" whereas a German in the same situation would probably speak of "aus einer Mücke einen Elefanten machen" [to make an elephant out of a gnat] (Spalding 1963:624) or "aus einem Furz einen Donnerschlag machen" [to make a thunderclap out of a fart] (Spalding 1960:485).

Presumably each reader familiar with a non-German culture can judge for himself whether this other culture evinces the same infatuation with scatological allusions that German culture does. All cultures surely have some scatological idioms and humor in the same way that every society imposes some kind of toilet training on its infants. While it is true that some Americans may say "shit" and Frenchmen say "merde," one does not find anything like the infinite variety of metaphorical anal expressions which can be shown to be traditional throughout Germany.

I doubt very much that many if any cultures can match German culture with respect to anality. From the countless proverbs, riddles, latrinalia verses, jokes, and folk poetry, we can see a consistent pattern. It is a pattern which can account for Luther's inspiration in the privy as well as Mozart's canons on the LMIA text. It is a pattern which is reflected in details as diverse as the construction of the German toilet, the curious figure of the "Dukatenscheisser," and the insidious iconography of the Judensau. It is a pattern found in German literature from Dedekind's *Grobianus* and Grimmelshausen's *Simplicius Simplicissimus* to Böll's *Group Portrait with Lady* and Grass's *The Flounder*.

What about the issue of German regionalism? This is a legitimate theoretical question, but I do not believe that genuine regional differences argue against the thesis that anality is a distinctive feature of German national character. As a matter of fact, some of the folklore of and about regionalism makes this very point far more eloquently than I can. A classic example of German latrinalia reveals how regionalism and anality can be combined. The following four verses appeared on the wall of a railroad bathroom in May of 1880 (Luedecke 1907:318; cf. Anon. 1908:272–273; Ihm 1912:496; and Collofino 1939:546):

Ein jeder, der hier scheissen will,	Anyone who shits here
muss sich ein wenig sputen,	has to hurry up a little,
denn die Bahn gewährt hiezu	For the train gives
in Gnaden 5 Minuten.	only five minutes grace.
Ein Norddeutscher	A North German.
Der obiges geschrieben hat,	Whoever wrote the above
ist sicherlich aus Preussen,	is surely from Prussia
den wo es nichts zu fressen gibt,	Because where there is nothing to eat
da gibts auch nichts zu scheissen.	there is also nothing to shit.
Ein Süddeutscher.	A South German.
Wer Deutschlands Einheit sehen will,	Who seeks to see Germany's unity
braucht gar nicht viel zu wandern,	really doesn't need to wander very far
denn, wie man hier geschrieben sieht,	Because as one sees it written here
scheisst einer auf den andern.	Each one shits on the other.
Ein Österreicher.	An Austrian.
Ob Süd-, ob Nord-, ob Österr-Deutsch	Whether South or North German or Austrian
Ihr Deutschen müsst doch raufen,	You Germans always quarrel with one another
drum scheiss ich euch als Streitobjekt	Therefore I shit you as a bone of contention
zur Teilung einen Haufen.	A heap for you to divide.
Ein Ungar.	A Hungarian.

Figure 13. A ceramic tile pokes fun at the Swabians. (Courtesy of Dr. Henry Gibbons, III.)

The pretended delineation of regional characteristics in scatological terms appears to be an ongoing tradition. A ceramic tile purchased in a little village store in Münchigen (outside Stuttgart) in 1978 entitled "Lied der Schwaben" pokes fun at the Swabians, using many of the most popular anal allusions (See figure 13).

If regionalism is not a decisive factor with respect to anality, what about German-speaking people outside of Germany proper? I believe that the traits described for the Germans apply to a varying degree to German-speaking peoples anywhere. Thus the scatological constellation of traits may well apply in part or in toto to Austrians, Swiss-Germans, Alsatians, German-Americans, etc. One may also expect to find parallels to some extent in Dutch culture and perhaps to a lesser extent even in Scandinavian and Anglo-American cultures. A piece of evidence suggesting that Germans themselves may recognize a similar tendency in Holland among other countries comes from one of the numerous joking novelty items based on a scatological theme. A coupon good for one shit in the woods remarks that the ticket is valid only for the Benelux countries and Germany.

Alsatian, as most people know, is a German dialect, not a French one, reminding us of the continuing Germanic nature of much of the population residing in this area of modern-day France. The late Jean-Paul Sartre in his autobiographical account *The Words* speaks of his Alsatian grandparents, the Schweitzers (related to Albert Schweitzer). He specifically bothered to mention how the men "told each other scatological jokes in the provincial dialect" and how "The Schweitzers were fond of crude words which, though belittling the body in very Christian fashion, manifested their broad acceptance of the natural functions" (1964:11, 12). Sartre had some rather vivid memories of his grandfather: "For years my grandfather rode me up and down on his leg and sang: 'Riding upon my bidet, when it trots, it leaves a fart,' and I would laugh with shame." Dandling rhymes are a standard genre of folklore, but it is significant that the one Sartre's Alsatian grandfather en-

147

joyed was anal erotic in theme. Sartre also recalled that his grandfather's "table-talk resembled that of Luther....He related the life of Saint Marie Alacoque, who licked up the excrement of sick persons with her tongue" (1964:57, 99). From the perspective provided by the present investigation, Sartre's Alsatian grandfather Charles Schweitzer was very much in (national) character.

Similarities between German and Swiss-German character might be found also. One psychoanalytically oriented study found that in the case of both Germans and Swiss, the mother's principal pedagogical efforts in the later phases of infancy "are directed primarily at training the child to comply with the socially desirable performance norms of neatness and cleanliness" which derive from the "necessary" sphincter training. However, it was suggested that whereas the training given by the German mother tends to encourage anal-aggressive attitudes, that given by the Swiss mother promotes anal-retentive—a distinction which I should think if valid might illuminate the positive attitude toward thrift in Switzerland and the high status of banking in that country (Parin and Parin-Matthey 1978:108, 118n.7).

If there is truly such a thing as national character, the question arises as to whether it remains stable over time. Louis L. Snyder in *Roots of German Nationalism* claims (1978:289) that "One of the few certainties in the study of national character is the dictum that national character is by no means fixed and permanent. The character of a people accurately reflects the era in which they live and it may undergo change under the impact of historical development." He then proceeds to suggest that the passive Germans of the eighteenth-century were transformed in the nineteenth-century into the Prussian image: "discipline, thoroughness, obedience, pedantry, punctuality, love of decoration and titles, respect for the military," an image which led to the two world wars. Late in the twentieth-century, German national character has been altered by exposure to Western democracy, Snyder argues. While not denying the possibility of national character's changing from one century to another, I submit that the array of evidence from both German folklore and literature supports the contrary view, namely, the continuity of German national character with respect to anality. The penchant for scatological imagery has remained remarkably constant over time.

Some writers on national character are sceptical about what has been termed the "toilet seat" school of psychology (Platt 1961:106), but it is difficult to see how such sceptics could possibly deny the emphasis on toilet seats in Germany for the past several centuries at least. I do wish to stress, however, that I am not claiming that German anal eroticism is necessarily *caused* by severe or early toilet training or by centuries of swaddling accompanied by infrequent changes of the swaddling clothes. It is always dangerous to seek single monolithic causes of complex phenomena. And besides, there is an inevitable logical flaw in assuming that any one element of a cultural whole is necessarily prior to all other elements in that culture. With respect to toilet training and swaddling, all I am suggesting is a structural parallel or isomorphism with adult personality characteristics. I submit German toilet training is consistent with the adult concern for cleanliness and order. Toilet training does not exist in a cultural vacuum. It is, after all, adults who impose toilet training regimes upon infants. So even if one were wont to argue that toilet training were critical with respect to the formation of adult personality, the argument becomes essentially circular. Adults impose toilet training; toilet training affects the nature of adult personality. The final formula would be: adults cause adult personality. Culture is a whole and it is always an arbitrary decision to single out one portion of the whole to analyze. On the other hand, I also think that the analysis of a portion may assist in the analysis of the whole to the extent that microcosms and macrocosms share common structural patterns.

Even if for the sake of argument one wished to claim that swaddling and toilet training were especially influential with respect to the development of personality characteristics in a given culture, that would not rule out the possibility of change. National character is not innate but rather acquired through exposure to whatever culture in which an individual spends his earliest, formative years. Inasmuch as German infants are no longer swaddled and toilet training may become less strict, it is perfectly possible that German character may change or be changing. In any case, national character is not indelible. What is learned can be unlearned and what has not been learned can be learned. German readers of this essay, if persuaded of its validity, might be moved to examine their own attitudes towards orderliness, for example. One of the avowed aims of folklorists is to make conscious what has hitherto been largely unconscious. If peoples have national character, they may or may not be aware of all the facets of that character. I believe that the folklore of a people reflects that people's character and that is why I have tried to examine German-speaking people through their own folklore.

Finally, I want to stress my conviction that the anal personality traits inherent in German national character are neither good nor evil per se. One could easily argue that the amassing of data, examining it, classifying it, etc. are the sine qua non of scholarship in many disciplines, including folkloristics. The art of the footnote, the building of bibliographies, the engineering of encyclopaedias surely have a respected place in modern academic life. But these same traits may just as well be used for ill. It is one thing for a student of incinerator design to say (Small 1971:122) that "A new generation of refuse incinerators has made West Germany the leader in the technology of solid waste disposal"; it is quite another for an earlier version of that technology to be tapped to promote genocide in order to make Germany Judenrein. So the same impulse may result in a Mozart canon and an Auschwitz. Immanuel Kant may have unwittingly provided one of the most apt metaphors for expressing the range of alternatives for the German's anal erotic proclivities. In a passage of his *Träume eines Geistersehers* written in 1766, Kant wrote: "Der scharfsichtige Hudibras hätte uns allein das Ratsel auflösen können, denn nach seiner Meinung: *wenn ein hypochondrischer Wind in den Eingeweiden tobet, so kommt es darauf an, welche Richtung er nimmt, geht er abwärts, so wird daraus ein Furz, steigt er aber aufwärts, so ist es eine Erscheinung oder eine heilige Eingebung*" [Only shrewd Hudibras could have solved the riddle because in his opinion: If a hypochondriacal wind storms in your bowels, it all depends which direction it takes. Should it go downwards, so a fart comes therefrom, but should it climb upwards, so it is a vision or holy inspiration] (Kant 1960:959–960).

The alternatives and the mixture of these alternatives—farts and inspirational visions—are part of German national character. Supposedly, anal erotic character can lead to either sadism or sentimentality or a combination of both (La Barre

1945:340, 326; cf. Rubenstein 1966:38). I am reminded of a folk definition of Germans offered by a Russian Jewish woman in New York in the early 1930s which beautifully encapsulates the strange combination of imputed cruelty and gushing sentiment: "A German is the kind of person who will pull the wings off a butterfly and then cry because it can no longer fly." To be sure, this is an example of national stereotype, not national character. Nevertheless, it may be well worth comparing the content of national stereotype traditions with the results of attempts to define national character (cf. Dundes 1975).

It is not enough to identify national character. One must analyze it so as to be better able to understand one's own national or ethnic identity as well as the national or ethnic identity of others. We live in a world where the daily increasing speed of travel and communication makes nearly all the peoples of the world neighbors to some degree. Unfortunately, our understanding of the cultural differences in personalities of the peoples of the world has not kept pace with advances in technology. Yet all the scientific advances in technology imaginable will not by themselves ensure peace and prosperity for the peoples of the earth. Without comparable insights in the study of national character and psychologies, we are destined to continue to live in constant fear of the threat of war and man's seemingly endless inhumanity to fellow man. Folklore represents a potential source for the serious study of national character and national psychologies, an unrivalled source whose potential has not been sufficiently utilized. If I have learned anything from this exercise, it has been that folklore expresses in direct, uncensored form the basic truths about a people and these truths are said by the people for the people. It is not I who is claiming that the German love of order may stem from a love of ordure—it is in the folklore. It is not I who am suggesting that to the famous three K's of the World War II slogan: Kinder, Kirche, Küche [children, church, kitchen] might be added a fourth: Kaka (Kacke) or Kot—it is in the folklore. It is the Germans themselves in their own folklore who have said all along that life is like a chickencoop ladder. And if the Germans are right, then they—and perhaps we— had better watch their step.

NOTES

1. In contemporary Germany both eating and drinking are often discussed with specific reference to the digestive process. Food and drink are typically adjudged healthy (gesund) so long as they aid in the prompt elimination of wastes from the intestinal tract. Liquids such as beer, wine, and coffee are deemed to have a positive effect insofar as they activate the intestines and thereby promote a flushing or cleaning out of the system. Foods are classified with respect to their impact. Some cause "Verstopfung," a clogging effect, that is, constipation; some are neutral, while others induce "Durchfall," a falling through, or diarrhea. Generally speaking, all starchy foods, such as noodles, potatoes, and white bread, are thought to lead to "Verstopfung." At the dinner table, someone eating too much of these foods might be warned against this action on the grounds that he will suffer from constipation the next day. It is believed that eating vegetables and fruit can counteract the ill effects of eating "Verdauungshemenden" (things blocking or inhibiting the digestive process), but such foods may cause diarrhea. If someone consumed an excessive number of apples or citrus fruits, he might be admonished accordingly. No doubt certain foods have physiological influences on the elimination cycle. What is significant here is that there is a conscious awareness of these influences and that it may serve as a common topic of dinner table conversation in German culture.

2. A children's rhyme collected in West Berlin in 1960 (Borneman 1976a:164 cf. Vetten) demonstrates the fecal association of the color:

Nichts ist ewig,	Nothing is eternal
Nichts ist gross!	Nothing is grand!
Auch das Braune	Even the brown
Wird man los!	One gets rid of.

BIBLIOGRAPHY

Aarne, Antti and Stith Thompson. 1961. *The Types of the Folktale*. FF Communications 184. Helsinki: Academia Scientiarum Fennica.

Abraham, Karl. 1953. "Contributions to the Theory of the Anal Character." *Selected Papers on Psychoanalysis*. New York: Basic Books, pp. 370–392.

Adler, Alfred. 1911. "Erotische Kinderspiele." *Anthropophyteia Jahrbücher*, 8:256–258.

Alderheiden, W. 1929. "Das Frankfurter Gassenkind." Friedrich S. Krauss, ed. *Das Minnelied des Deutsches Land- und Stadtvolkes*. Beiwerke Zum Studium der Anthropophyteia 9. Leipzig: Ethnologischer Verlag. pp. 231–259.

Alexander, W.M. 1966. *Johann Georg Hamann:* Philosophy and Faith. The Hague: Martinus Nijhoff.

Amrain, K. 1908. "Deutsche sprichwörtliche Redensarten." *Anthropophyteia Jahrbücher*, 5:184–186.

Anderson, Emily. 1938. *The Letters of Mozart & His Family*. 3 vols. London: Macmillan.

Andreas-Salomé, Lou. 1916. " 'Anal' und 'Sexual' " *Imago*, 4:249–273.

Anon. 1867. "Female Education in Germany." *Cornhill Magazine*, 15:354–365.

——1908. "Bahnhofabortinschriften." *Anthropophyteia Jahrbücher*, 5:272–273.

——1912. "Skatologische Inschriften." *Anthropophyteia Jahrbücher*, 9:505–507.

————1968. *Volks-Erotik*. Hanau/Main: Verlag Karl Schustek.

————1970. *Bibliotheca Scatologica*. Leipzig: Zentralantiquariat der Deutschen Demokratischen Republik.

————1976. "Wie sauber sind die Deutschen?" *Bild der Wissenschaft*, 12:126–144.

————1979a. *Dir gehört der Arsch versohlt: Die erotische Freude am Popoklatschen*. Cologne: Argospress.

————1979b. "Doctors of the Death Camps." *Time*, 113, no.26 (June 25, 1979):68.

————1979c. "Leading from Strength." *Time*, 112, no.24 (June 11, 1979):26–35.

Apitzsch, George. 1909. "Rätselfragen deutscher Seefahrer." *Anthropophyteia Jahrbücher*, 6:412.

Azrin, Nathan H. and Richard M. Foxx. 1974. *Toilet Training in Less Than A Day*. New York: Pocket Books.

Bailey, George. 1974. *Germans: Biography of an Obsession*. New York: Avon.

Barker, Ernest. 1948. *National Character and the Factors in its Formation*. London: Methuen.

Bateson, Gregory. 1953. "An Analysis of the Nazi Film *Hitlerjunge Quex.*" *The Study of Culture at a Distance*. Margaret Mead and Rhoda Métraux, eds. Chicago: University of Chicago Press. pp. 302–314.

Bauer, Wilhelm A. and Otto Erich Deutsch. 1962. *Mozart: Briefe und Aufzeichnungen*. Band II: 1777–1779. Kassel: Bärenreiter.

Bebel, Heinrich. 1907. *Heinrich Bebels Schwänke*. Albert Wesselski, ed. Erster Band. Munich and Leipzig: Georg Müller.

Beloff, Halla. 1957. "The Structure and Origin of the Anal Character." *Genetic Psychology Monographs*, 55:141–172.

Benedict, Ruth. 1949. "Child-Rearing in Certain European Countries." *American Journal of Orthopsychiatry*, 19:342–350.

Berliner, Friedrich W. 1909. "Rätselfragen aus Berlin." *Anthropophyteia Jahrbücher*, 6:412–413.

Bishop, Frances V. 1967. "The Anal Character: A Rebel in the Dissonance Family." *Journal of Personality and Social Psychology*, 6:23–36.

Blinkiewicz, B. 1911. "Erzählungen aus Russisch-Polen." *Anthropophyteia Jahrbücher*, 8:332–348.

Blümml, E. K. 1908. "Schamperlieder-Deutsche Volkslieder des 16–19 Jahrhunderts." *Futilates:* Beiträge zur Volkskundlichen Erotik, Vol. 1. Vienna: Privatdruck.

Blumauer, Alois. 1884. *Sämmtliche Werke,* Vol. 1. Vienna: Verlag von Moritz Stern.

Boas, Franz. 1935. *Kwakiutl Culture as Reflected in Mythology.* Memoirs of the American Folklore Society 28. New York: G.E. Stechert.

Böll, Heinrich. 1973. *Group Portrait with Lady.* New York: McGraw-Hill.

Bolte, Johannes and Georg Polivka. 1913. *Anmerkungen zu den Kinder-und Hausmärchen der Brüder Grimm.* Vol. I. Leipzig: Dieterich' sche Verlagsbuchhandlung.

Borneman, Ernest. 1971. *Sex im Volksmund:* Die sexuelle Umgangssprache des deutschen Volkes. Reinbek bei Hamburg: Rowohlt Verlag.

——1973. *Unsere Kinder im Spiegel ihrer Lieder, Reime, Verse und Rätsel. Studien zur Befreiung des Kindes I.* Olten: Walter-Verlag.

——1974. *Die Umwelt des Kindes im Spiegel seiner 'verbotenen' Lieder, Reime, Verse und Rätsel. Studien zur Befreiung des Kindes II.* Olten: Walter-Verlag.

——1976a. *Die Welt der Erwachsenen in den 'verbotenen' Reimen deutschsprachiger Stadtkinder. Studien zur Befreiung des Kindes III.* Olten: Walter-Verlag.

——1976b. *The Psychoanalysis of Money.* New York: Urizen Books.

Bosmajian, Hamida. 1979. *Metaphors of Evil: Contemporary German Literature and the Shadow of Nazism.* Iowa City: University of Iowa Press.

Bourke, John G. 1891. *Scatalogic Rites of All Nations.* Washington: W. H. Lowdermilk.

Brecht, Bertolt. 1971. *Collected Plays.* Ralph Manheim and John Wilett, eds. Vol. 1. New York: Vintage.

Brenneisl, Leonhard. 1908. "Abortinschriften aus der Temesvarer Kolonie." *Anthropophyteia Jahrbücher,* 5:272.

Brewster, Paul G. 1942. *American Nonsinging Games.* Norman: University of Oklahoma Press.

Brodersen, Arvid. 1957. "National Character: An Old Problem Re-Examined." *Diogenes,* 20:84–102.

Brophy, Brigid. 1964. *Mozart the Dramatist*. London: Faber and Faber.

Brown, Norman O. 1959. *Life Against Death: The Psychoanalytical Meaning of History*. Middletown: Wesleyan University Press.

Buckle, Donald. 1953. "The Instinctual Basis of Anal Erotism: A Note on the Relations Between Ethology and Psycho-Analytic Theory." *British Journal of Medical Psychology*, 26:289–294.

Burke, Kenneth. 1963. "The Thinking of the Body: Comments on the Imagery of Catharsis in Literature. *Psychoanalytic Review*, 50:375–418.

Caro Baroja, Julio. 1951. "Sobre psicología étnica." *Revista de Dialectologia y Tradiciones Popolares*, 7:254–265.

——1970. *El Mito del Caracter Nacional. Meditaciones a Contrapelo*. Madrid: Seminarios y Ediciones.

Centers, Richard. 1969. "The Anal Character and Social Severity in Attitudes." *Journal of Projective Techniques and Personality Assessment*, 33:501–506.

Chapman, Charlotte Gower. 1971. *Milocca: A Sicilian Village*. Cambridge: Schenkman.

Clark, Robert T., Jr. 1969. *Herder: His Life and Thought*. Berkeley and Los Angeles: University of California Press.

Clemens, Samuel L. 1880. *A Tramp Abroad*. Hartford: American Publishing Company.

Coleridge, Samuel Taylor. 1912. *The Complete Poetical Works of Samuel Taylor; Coleridge*. Vol. 1. Ernest Hartley Coleridge, ed. Oxford: Clarendon Press.

Collofino. 1939. *Non Olet oder Die heiteren Tischgespräche des Collofino über den Orbis Cacatus*. Cologne: Privatdruck.

Coturnix. 1979. *Erbauliche Enzy-Clo-Pädie*: Kulturgeschichte eines verschwiegenen Örtchens. Wien: Meyster Verlag.

Dennis, Wayne. 1940. "Infant Reaction to Restraint: An Evaluation of Watson's Theory." *Transactions of the New York Academy of Sciences*, Series 2. 2:202–218.

deMause, Lloyd. 1975. "The Evolution of Childhood." *The History of Childhood*. Lloyd deMause, ed. New York: Harper Torchbooks. pp. 1–73.

Des Pres, Terrence. 1977. *The Survivor: An Anatomy of Life in the Death Camps*. New York: Pocket Books.

Dicks, H. V. 1950. "Some Psychological Studies of the German Character." *Psychological Factors of Peace and War.* T. H. Pear, ed. London: Hutchinson & Co., pp. 193–218.

Diepgen, P. 1953. *Das Analzäpfchen in der Geschichte der Therapie.* Stuttgart: Georg Thieme Verlag.

Domhoff, G. William. 1970. "Two Luthers: The Traditional and the Heretical in Freudian Psychology." *Psychoanalytic Review,* 57:5–17.

Duijker, H. C. J. and N. H. Fridja. 1960. *National Character and National Stereotypes.* Amsterdam: North-Holland Publishing Co.

Dundes, Alan. 1975. "Slurs International: Folk Comparisons of Ethnicity and National Character." *Southern Folklore Quarterly,* 39:15–38.

Dunning, Albert. 1973. "Mozarts Kanons: Eine Studie." *Mozart-Jahrbuch* 1971–72:227–240.

Ellis, Havelock. 1920. *Studies in the Psychology of Sex.* Vol. V. Erotic Symbolism. Philadelphia: F. A. Davis Company.

Ende, Aurel. 1979–1980. "Battering and Neglect: Children in Germany, 1860–1978." *Journal of Psychohistory,* 7:249–279.

Englisch, Paul. 1928a. *Anrüchiges und Allzumenschliches: Einblicke in das Kapitel PFUI.* Stuttgart: Julius Püttmann.

Englisch, Paul. 1928b. *Das Skatologische Element in Literatur, Kunst und Volksleben.* Stuttgart: Julius Püttman.

Enzensberger, Christian. 1968. *Grösserer Versuch über den Schmutz.* Munich: Carl Hanser Verlag.

Ergang, Robert. 1931. *Herder and the Foundations of German Nationalism.* New York: Columbia University Press.

Erikson, Erik H. 1958. *Young Man Luther:* A Study in Psychoanalysis and History. New York: W. W. Norton.

Farber, Maurice L. 1950. "The Problem of National Character: A Methodological Analysis. *Journal of Psychology,* 30:307–315.

Favezza, Armando R. 1974. "A Critical Review of Studies of National Character: A Psychiatric-Anthropological Interface." *Journal of Operational Psychiatry,* 6:3–30.

Feldhaus, Franz Maria. 1921. *Ka-Pi-Fu und andere verschämte Dinge.* Berlin: Privatdruck.

Ferenczi, Sandor. 1956. "The Ontogenesis of the Interest in Money." *Sex in Psycho-Analysis.* New York: Dover, pp. 269–279.

Flögel, Karl Friedrich. 1862. *Geschichte des Grotesk-Komischen.* Leipzig: Verlag von Adolf Werl.

Förster, Hans. 1912. "Sprichwort aus Schaumburg-Lippe." *Anthropophyteia Jahrbücher,* 9:480.

Freud, Sigmund. 1938. *The Basic Writings of Sigmund Freud.* New York: Modern Library.

——1959. "Character and Anal Erotism." *Collected Papers.* Vol. 2. New York: Basic Books. pp. 45–50.

Freud, Sigmund and D. E. Oppenheim. 1958. *Dreams in Folklore.* New York: International Universities Press.

Freudenthal, Herbert. 1955. "Vorbemerkungen zu einer deutschen Volkscharakterkunde." *Zeitschrift für Volkskunde,* 52:39–75.

Friedenwald, Julius and Samuel Morrison. 1940. "The History of the Enema with Some Notes on Related Procedures." *Bulletin of the History of Medicine,* 8:68–114, 239–276.

Friedman, Albert B. 1968. "The Scatological Rites of Burglars. *Western Folklore,* 27:171–179.

Fromm, Erich. 1973. *The Anatomy of Human Destructiveness.* New York: Holt, Rinehart and Winston.

Fuchs, Eduard. 1921. *Die Juden in der Karikatur:* Ein Beitrag zur Kulturgeschichte. Munich: Albert Langen.

Fuchs, Toni. 1969. *Die Reinlichkeitserziehung im Kanton Appenzell-Innerrhoden (Schweiz)* Zürich: Juris.

Gennep, Arnold van. 1922. *Traité comparatif des Nationalités.* I. Les Éléments Extérieurs de la Nationalité. Paris: Payot.

Gerhardt, F. von. 1908. "Breslauer Abortinschriften." *Anthropophyteia Jahrbücher,* 5:270.

Gilbert, G. M. 1947. *Nuremberg Diary.* New York: Farrar, Straus.

Ginsberg, M. 1942. "National Character." *British Journal of Psychology,* 32:183–205.

——1960. "German Views of German Mentality." *Essays in Sociology and Social Philosophy,* Vol. 2. *Reason and Unreason in Society.* New York: Macmillan, pp. 156–176.

Godelück, William. 1906a. "Erotische und skatologische Kinder- und Jugendreime." *Anthropophyteia Jahrbücher,* 3:218–243.

———1906b. "Sprichwörter und sprichwörtliche Redensarten aus dem El-sass." *Anthropophyteia Jahrbücher,* 3:132–143.

Goethe, Johann Wolfgang von. 1941. *Faust.* Carlyle F. Mac Intyre, trans. Norfolk: New Directions.

———1949. *Goethe's Autobiography: Poetry and Truth from My Own Life.* R. O. Moon, trans. Washington: Public Affairs Press.

———1962. *Italian Journey.* New York: Pantheon.

———1964. "Hanswursts Hochzeit oder Der Lauf der Welt: Ein mikrokos-misches Drama." *Poetische Werke,* Berliner Ausgabe 5. Berlin: Auf-bau-Verlag. pp. 488–492.

———1965. *Götz von Berlichingen.* New York: Frederick Ungar.

———1970. *Aus Meinem Leben, Dichtung und Wahrheit.* Berlin: Akademie Verlag.

Gorer, Geoffrey. 1949. "Development of the Swaddling Hypotheses." Geof-frey Gorer and John Rickman, *The People of Great Russia:* A Psycho-logical Study. London: The Cresset Press. pp. 197–222.

Grass, Günter. 1962. *The Tin Drum.* New York: Pantheon.

1978. *The Flounder.* New York: Fawcett Crest.

Greenacre, Phyllis. 1944. "Infant Reactions to Restraint: Problems in the Fate of Infantile Aggression. *American Journal of Orthopsychiatry,* 14:204–218.

Grimmelshausen, Christoffel von. 1964. *Simplicius Simplicissimus.* Lon-don: John Calder.

Grinstein, Alexander. 1968. *On Sigmund Freud's Dreams.* Detroit: Wayne State University Press.

Hand, Wayland D. 1980. "*Padepissers* and *Wekschissers: A Folk Medical Inquiry into the Cause of Styes.*" Kenneth S. Goldstein and Neil V. Rosenberg, eds. *Folklore Studies in Honour of Herbert Halpert.* St. Johns: Memorial University of Newfoundland. pp. 211–223.

Hašek, Jaroslav. 1974. *The Good Soldier: Švejk.* New York: Crowell.

Hayman, John G. 1971–1972. "Notions on National Characters in the Eighteenth Century." *Huntington Library Quarterly,* 35:1–17.

Hecht, Ben. 1964. *Letters from Bohemia.* Garden City: Doubleday.

Heimann, Paula. 1962. "Notes on the Anal Stage." *International Journal of Psycho-Analysis,* 43:406–414.

Heimpel, J. 1912. "Das Lied von der Reinlichkeit." *Anthropophyteia Jahrbücher*, 9:502.

Hellwig, Albert. 1905. "Der grumus merdae der Einbrecher." *Anthropophyteia Jahrbücher*, 2:442–444.

Helm, Charles. 1979. "The German Concept of Order: The Social and Physical Setting." *Journal of Popular Culture*, 13:67–80.

Hermand, Jost. 1971. *Stänker und Weismacher: Zur Dialektik eines Affekts.* Texte Metzler 18. Stuttgart: J. M. Metzlersche Verlagsbuchhandlung.

Hertz, Friedrich. 1925. "Die allgemeinen Theorien vom Nationalcharakter." *Archiv für Sozialwissenschaft und Sozialpolitik*, 54:1–35, 657–715.

Hildesheimer, Wolfgang. 1977. *Mozart.* Frankfurt: Suhrkamp.

Hill, A. B. 1976. "Methodological Problems in the Use of Factor Analysis: A Critical Review of The Experimental Evidence for the Anal Character." *British Journal of Medical Psychology*, 49:145–159.

Himmlisch, Wetti. 1907. *Leben, Meinungen und Wirken.* Leipzig: Deutsche Verlagsactiengesellschaft.

Hitler, Adolf. 1953. *Hitler's Secret Conversations 1941–1944.* New York: Farrar, Straus.

Hoffmann-Krayer, E. and Hanns Bächtold-Stäubli, eds. 1927–1942. *Handwörterbuch des deutschen Aberglaubens.* 10 vols. Berlin and Leipzig: Walter de Gruyter.

Hofstätter, Peter R. 1966–1967. "Was Deutsche fur 'Deutsch' Halten." *Eckart-Jahrbuch 1966/67*:29–46.

Holt, Tonie and Valmai Holt. 1977. *Till the Boys Come Home: The Picture Postcards of the First World War.* Newtown Square, Pa.: Deltiologists of America.

Hudson, Charles and Helen Phillips. 1968. "Rousseau and the Disappearance of Swaddling among Western Europeans." *Essays on Medical Anthropology*, Thomas Weaver, ed. Athens: University of Georgia Press, pp. 13–22.

Hume, David. 1882. "Of National Characters." *Essays: Moral, Political and Literary.* Vol. 1. London: Longmans, Green, pp. 244–258.

Huschka, Mabel. 1942. "The Child's Response to Coercive Bowel Training." *Psychosomatic Medicine*, 4:301–308.

Ihm, H. 1912. "Skatologisches aus der Maingegend." *Anthropophyteia Jahrbücher*, 9:493–500.

Inkeles, Alex and Daniel J. Levinson. 1969. "National Character: The Study of Modal Personality and Sociocultural Systems." *The Handbook of Social Psychology.* Gardner Lindzey and Elliot Aronson, eds. 2nd ed. Vol. 4. Reading, Mass.: Addison-Wesley Publishing Company. pp. 418–506.

International Military Tribunal. 1947. *Trial of the Major War Criminals.* Vol. 7. Official Text in the English Language. Proceedings 5 February 1946–19 February 1946. Nuremberg.

Jeep, Ernst. 1896. "Eulenspiegel." Thomas Murner, *Die Gäuchmatt.* ed. Wilhelm Uhl. Leipzig: B. G. Teubner. pp. 268–288.

Jones, Ernest. 1961. "Anal-Erotic Character Traits." *Papers on Psychoanalysis.* Boston: Beacon Press. pp. 413–437.

Jong, Erica. 1974. *Fear of Flying.* New York: Signet.

Jung, C. G. 1973. *Memories, Dreams, Reflections.* New York: Pantheon.

Jurreit, Marielouise. 1969. "Alles über Scheisse." *twen* (December, 1969);118–123, 140.

Kahl, Inge and E. Ehler. 1970. "Einläufe und Zäpfchen aus dem beginnenden 18. Jahrundert in heutiger Sicht." *Pharmazeutische Praxis,* 11:258–260.

Kahler, Erich. 1974. *The Germans.* Princeton: Princeton University Press.

Kamenetsky, Christa. 1972. "Folklore as a Political Tool in Nazi Germany." *Journal of American Folklore,* 85:221–235.

——1977. "Folktale and Ideology in the Third Reich." *Journal of American Folklore,* 90:168–178.

Kant, Immanuel. 1880. *Anthropologie in pragmatischer Hinsicht.* Leipzig: Erich Koschny.

——1960. *Werke in Sechs Banden.* Wilhelm Weischedel, ed. Band I. Wiesbaden: Insel-Verlag.

Kaufmann, David. 1890. "La Truie de Wittenberg." *Revue des Études Juives,* 20:269–274.

Kaufman, Walter, ed. 1968. *Basic Writings of Nietzsche.* New York: Modern Library.

Kecskemeti, Paul and Nathan Leites. 1947–1948. "Some Psychological Hypotheses on Nazi Germany." *Journal of Social Psychology,* 26:141–183; 27:91–117, 241–270; 28:141–164.

Kind, Alfred. 1950. *Die kallipygischen Reize.* Alfred Kind and Curt Moreck, *Gefilde der Lust.* Vienna: Verlag für Kulturforschung. pp. 199–351.

Kira, Alexander. 1976. *The Bathroom*. New York: Viking Press.

Kline, Paul. 1972. *Fact and Fantasy in Freudian Theory*. London: Methuen.

Klingner, Erich. 1912. *Luther und der deutsche Volksaberglaube*. *Palaestra* 56. Berlin: Mayer & Müller.

Kluckhohn, Clyde. 1962. *Culture and Behavior: The Collected Essays of Clyde Kluckhohn*. Richard Kluckhohn, ed. New York: Free Press.

Kraus, Ota and Erich Kulka. 1966. *The Death Factory: Document on Auschwitz*. Oxford: Pergamon Press.

Krauss, Friedrich S. and Karl Reiskel. 1905. "Rätsel und Rätselfragen niederösterreichischer Stadtleute." *Anthropophyteia Jahrbücher*, 2:26–60.

Kriegk, Georg Ludwig. 1840. *Schriften zur allgemeinen Erdkunde*. Leipzig: Verlag von Wilhelm Engelmann.

Krotus, Michael. 1970. *Klappentexte: Materialien zur Psychologie der Dichtung*. Freiburg: Pen Press.

Kubie, Lawrence S. 1937. "The Fantasy of Dirt." *Psychoanalytic Quarterly*, 6:388–425.

Kuehnelt-Leddihn, Erik von. 1950. "Réflexions sur le caractère national autrichien." *Revue de Psychologie des Peuples*, 5:269–298.

Kühlewein, Hermann. 1909. "Erotische Kinderreime aus Gross-Frankfurt." *Anthropophyteia Jahrbücher*, 6:400–401.

Kühlewein, H. and Joh. Koštiál and Lebrecht Kaufmann. 1910. "Die Erotik in der Lateinschule." *Anthropophyteia Jahrbücher*, 7:237–238.

La Barre, Weston. 1945. "Some Observations on Character Structure in the Orient: The Japanese." *Psychiatry*, 8:319–342.

Landauer, Karl. 1939. "Some Remarks on the Formation of the Anal-Erotic Character." *International Journal of Psycho-Analysis*, 20:418–425.

Langer, Walter C. 1972. *The Mind of Adolf Hitler: The Secret Wartime Report*. New York: Basic Books.

Laporte, Dominique. 1978. *Histoire de la Merde (Prologue)*. Paris: Christian Bourgois Éditeur.

Legman, G. 1968. *Rationale of the Dirty Joke: An Analysis of Sexual Humor*. New York: Grove Press.

——1975. *No Laughing Matter: Rationale of the Dirty Joke, Second Series*. Wharton, New Jersey: Breaking Point.

164

Leonhardt, W. 1911. "Die beiden ältesten Skatologika der deutschen Literatur." *Anthropophyteia Jahrbücher,* 8:400–406.

Lewin, Kurt. 1936. "Some Social-Psychological Differences Between the United States and Germany." *Character and Personality,* 4:265–293.

Lewis, Beth Irwin. 1971. *George Grosz:* Art and Politics in the Weimar Republic. Madison: University of Wisconsin Press.

Lichtenberg, Georg Christoph. 1959. *Selected Writings.* F.H. Mautner and H. Hatfield, eds. New York: Beacon.

Lieberman, William. 1946. "The Enema: Some Historical Notes," *Review of Gastroenterology,* 13:215–229.

Limbach, Alfred. 1980. *Der Furz.* Cologne: argos press.

Lind, Jakov. 1969. *Counting My Steps. An Autobiography.* London: Collier-Macmillan.

Lowie, Robert H. 1945. *The German People: A Social Portrait to 1914.* New York: Farrar & Rinehart.

——1954. *Toward Understanding Germany.* Chicago: University of Chicago Press.

Ludwig, Emil, 1938. "The German Mind." *Atlantic Monthly,* 161:255–263.

Luedecke, Hugo E. 1907. "Grundlagen der Skatologie." *Anthropophyteia Jahrbücher,* 4:316–327.

——1908. "Mitteldeutsche erotische Volkrätsel." *Anthropophyteia Jahrbücher,* 5:187–189.

——1912. "Skatologische Inschriften." *Anthropophyteia Jahrbücher,* 9:504.

Luther, Martin. 1911. *The Table Talk of Martin Luther.* William Hazlitt, ed. London: G. Bell.

——1966. "Against Hanswurst." *Luther's Works,* Vol. 41, Church and Ministry, III. Philadelphia: Fortress Press. pp. 185–256.

——1971. "On the Jews and Their Lies." *Luther's Works,* Vol. 47, The Christian in Society, IV. Philadelphia: Fortress Press. pp. 137–306.

Lynn, R. 1971. *Personality and National Character.* Oxford: Pergamon Press.

Maas, Walther. 1960, "Nationalcharakterstudien." *Ostdeutsche Wissenschaft,* 7:3–22.

Manchester, William. 1968. *The Arms of Krupp.* Boston: Little, Brown.

Mann, Thomas. 1930. *A Man and his Dog.* New York: Alfred A. Knopf.

———1946. "Germany and the Germans." *Yale Review,* 35:223–241.

Markowitz, Joel. 1969. *The Psychodynamic Evolution of Groups.* New York: Vantage Press.

Martindale, Don, ed. 1967. *National Character in the Perspective of the Social Sciences, Annals of the American Academy of Political and Social Science,* 370:1–63.

Masur, Gerhard. 1975. "Der Nationale Charakter als Problem der Deutschen Geschichte." *Historische Zeitschrift,* 221:603–622.

Mayhew, Henry. 1864. *German Life and Manners as Seen in Saxony at the Present Day.* 2 vols. London: Wm. H. Allen.

Mead, Margaret. 1951. "The Study of National Character." *The Policy Sciences: Recent Developments in Scope and Method.* Daniel Lerner and Harold D. Lasswell, eds. Stanford: Stanford University Press. pp. 70-85.

———1954. "The Swaddling Hypothesis: Its Reception." *American Anthropologist,* 56:395–409.

Menninger, William C. 1943. "Characterologic and Symptomatic Expressions Related to the Anal Phase of Psychosexual Development." *Psychoanalytic Quarterly,* 12:161–193.

Merrill, Bruce R. 1951. "Childhood Attitudes Toward Flatulence and Their Possible Relation to Adult Character." *Psychoanalytic Quarterly,* 20:550–564.

Métraux, Rhoda. 1955. "Parents and Children: An Analysis of Contemporary German Child-Care and Youth-Guidance Literature." *Childhood in Contemporary Cultures.* Margaret Mead and Martha Wolfenstein, eds. Chicago: University of Chicago Press. pp. 204–228.

Meyer, Richard M. 1892–1893. "German Character as Reflected in the National Life and Literature." *International Journal of Ethics,* 3:202–242.

Mieder, Wolfgang. 1978. "Das Wort 'Shit' und seine lexikographische Erfassung." *Sprachspiegel,* 34:76-79.

Montague, J. F. 1934. "History and Appraisal of the Enema." *Medical Record,* 139:91-93, 142-145, 194-195, 245-247, 297-299, 458-460.

Montaigne, Michel Eyquem de. 1927. *The Essays of Montaigne.* 2 vols. London: Oxford University Press.

Moog, Willy. 1916. "Kants völkerpsychologische Beobachtungen über die Charaktere der europäischen Nationen." *Vierteljahrsschrift für wissenschaftliche Philosophie und Soziologie*, 40:293–299.

More, Thomas. 1969. *The Complete Works of St. Thomas More*, Vol. 5, Responsio ad Lutherum. Part 1. John M. Headley, ed. New Haven: Yale University Press.

Müller, Carl, 1911. "Beiträge zur Skatologie." *Anthropophyteia Jahrbücher*, 8:398–399.

Müller-Freienfels, Richard. 1936. *The German: His Psychology & Culture: An Inquiry into Folk Character*. Los Angeles: New Symposion Press.

Müllerheim, Robert. 1904. *Die Wochenstube in der Kunst*. Stuttgart: Verlag von Ferdinand Enke.

Nett, Emily M. 1958. "An Evaluation of the National Character Concept in Sociological Theory." *Social Forces*, 36:297–303.

Nohain, Jean and F. Caradec. 1967. *Le Petomane, 1857–1945*. Los Angeles: Sherbourne Press.

Nurge, Ethel. 1975. "Some Depictions of German Cultural Character." *The New Ethnicity: Perspectives from Ethnology*. John W. Bennett, ed. St. Paul: West Publishing Co. pp. 217–257.

——1977. *Blue Light in the Village: Daily Life in a German Village in 1965–66*. Ann Arbor: University Microfilms International.

Oppenheimer, Paul, ed. 1972. *A Pleasant Vintage of Till Eulenspiegel*. Middletown: Wesleyan University Press.

Ouellette, William. 1975. *Fantasy Postcards*. Garden City: Doubleday.

Parin, Paul and Goldy Parin-Matthey, 1978. "The Swiss and Southern German Lower-Middle Class: An Ethno-psychoanalytic Study." *Journal of Psychological Anthropology*, 1:101–119.

Pfleiderer, Otto. 1892–1893. "The National Traits of the Germans as Seen in Their Religion." *International Journal of Ethics*, 3:1–39.

Platt, Washington. 1961. *National Character in Action—Intelligence Factors in Foreign Relations*. New Brunswick: Rutgers University Press.

Pollack, Herman. 1971. *Jewish Folkways in Germanic Lands (1648–1806): Studies in Aspects of Daily Life*. Cambridge: M.I.T. Press.

Polsterer, Josef. 1908. "Militaria," *Futilates*, 4:1–205.

Pops, Martin. 1982. "The Metamorphosis of Shit." *Salmagundi*, No. 56:26–61.

Praetorius, Numa. 1911. "Inschriften aus den Aborten eines süddeutschen Universitätgebaudes." *Anthropophyteia Jahrbücher,* 8:422–425.

Prugh, Dane G. 1954. "Childhood Experience and Colonic Disorder." *Annals of the New York Academy of Sciences,* 58:355–376.

Reid, T. B. W. 1967. "The Dirty End of the Stick." *Revue de Linguistique Romane,* 31:55–63.

Reik, Theodor. 1949. *The Unknown Murderer.* New York: International Universities Press.

Remarque, Erich Maria. 1958. *All Quiet on the Western Front.* New York: Fawcett.

Roberts, Warren E. 1958. *The Tale of the Kind and the Unkind Girls.* Berlin: Walter de Gruyter.

Röhrich, Lutz. 1967. *Erzählungen des Späten Mittelalters und Ihr Weiterleben in Literatur und Volksdichtung bis zur Gegenwart.* 2 vols. Bern and Munich: Francke Verlag.

Rollfinke, Dieter Jürgen. 1977. "Menschliche Kunst: A Study of Scatology in Modern German Literature." Doctoral dissertation. Johns Hopkins University.

Ross, W. Donald, Michael Hirt and Richard Kurtz. 1968. "The Fantasy of Dirt and Attitudes Toward Body Products." *Journal of Nervous and Mental Disease,* 146:303–309.

Rousseau, J. J. 1906. *Rousseau's Émile or Treatise on Education.* William H. Payne, trans. London: Sidney Appleton.

Rubenstein, Richard L. 1966. *After Auschwitz.* Indianapolis: Bobbs-Merrill.

Rühl, Ernst. 1904. *Grobianus in England. Palaestra 38.* Berlin: Mayer & Müller.

Rühmkorf, Peter. 1967. *Über das Volksvermögen: Exkurse in den literarischen Untergrund.* Reinbek bei Hamburg: Rowohlt Verlag.

——1972. *Die Jahre die Ihr kennt. Anfälle und Erinnerungen.* Reinbek bei Hamburg: Rowohlt Verlag.

Sabbath, Dan and Mandel Hall. 1977. *End Product: The First Taboo.* New York: Urizen Books.

Sartre, Jean-Paul. 1964. *The Words.* New York: George Braziller.

Schaffner, Bertram. 1948. *Father Land: A Study of Authoritarianism in the German Family.* New York: Columbia University Press.

Schalk, Adolph. 1971. *The Germans*. Englewood Cliffs: Prentice-Hall.

Scheidemann, Philipp. 1928. *Memoiren Eines Sozialdemokraten*. Erster Band. Dresden: Carl Reissner Verlag.

Schenk, Dr. 1912. "Skatologische Inschriften." *Anthropophyteia Jahrbücher*, 9:503–504.

Schertel, A. 1976. "Eine kleine Historie des Purgierens." *Therapie der Gegenwart*, 115:1796–1802.

Schertel, Ernst. 1929–1932. *Der Flagellantismus als literarisches Motiv: Eine literaturgeschichtlich-psychologische Untersuchung*. 4 vols. Leipzig: Parthenon-Verlag.

——1932a. *Der Erotische Komplex*. Band 1. *Gesäss-Erotik*. Berlin: Pergamon-Verlag.

——1932b. *Der Erotische Komplex*. Band 2. *Der Komplex der Flagellomanie*. Berlin: Pergamon-Verlag.

Schlichtegroll, Carl Felix von. 1909. "Onomastikon norddeutscher das Sexualleben betreffender Ausdrücke." *Anthropophyteia Jahrbücher*, 6:1–11.

Schnabel, Friedrich Erich. 1970. "Lieder gesammelt in Westfalen." *Das Geschlechtsleben des deutschen Volkes*. Friedrich S. Krauss, ed. Hanau: Verlag Karl Schustek. pp. 34–42.

Schopenhauer, Arthur. 1958. *The World as Will and Representation*. E. F. J. Payne, trans, Vol. 1. Indian Hills, Colorado: The Falcon's Wing Press.

Schramm, Heinz-Eugen. 1967. *L.m.i.A.: Des Ritters Gotz von Berlichingen denkwürdige Fensterrede*. Gerlingen: Koernersche Druckerei und Verlagsanstalt.

Schüz, E. 1877. "Volkstümliches." *Alemannia*, 4:273–274.

Schweigmann, Braunhard. 1970. "Die Poesie der Imponderabilien." *Das Geschlechtsleben des Deutschen Volkes*. Friedrich S. Krauss, ed. Hanau: Verlag Karl Schustek. pp. 114–139.

Sebald, Hans. 1961. "Studying National Character Through Comparative Content Analysis." *Social Forces*, 40:318–322.

Shachar, Isaiah. 1974. *The Judensau: A Medieval Anti-Jewish Motif and Its History*. London: The Warburg Institute.

Sidgwick, Mrs. Alfred. 1912. *Home Life in Germany*. New York: Macmillan.

Small, William E. 1971. *Third Pollution:* The National Problem of Solid Waste Disposal. New York: Praeger.

Snyder, Louis L. 1978. *Roots of German Nationalism.* Bloomington: Indiana University Press.

Spalding, Keith. 1952–1981. *An Historical Dictionary of German Figurative Usage.* Oxford: Basil Blackwell.

Spalding, K. 1958. "A Note on German *Dreck am Stecken."* *Archivum Linguisticum* 10:43–47.

Spencer, Robert F. 1965. "The German Paradox." *Journal of the Minnesota Academy of Science,* 32:160–182.

Spindler, George D. 1973. *Burgbach:* Urbanization and Identity in a German Village. New York: Holt, Rinehart and Winston.

Stein, Howard F. 1978. "The Slovak-American 'Swaddling Ethos': Homeostat for Family Dynamics and Cultural Continuity." *Family Process,* 17:31–45.

Storck, Karl. 1895. "Spruchgedichte und Volksbräuche aus der Vorderschweiz," *Zeitschrift des Vereins für Volkskunde,* 5:384–390.

Stuckenberg, J. H. W. 1882. *The Life of Immanuel Kant.* London: Macmillan.

Sydow, C. W. von. 1948. *Selected Papers on Folklore.* Laurits Bødker, ed. Copenhagen: Rosenkilde and Bagger.

Szalet, Leon. 1945. *Experiment "E":* A Report from an Extermination Laboratory. New York: Didier.

Tacitus. 1970. *The Agricola and the Germania.* New York: Penguin.

Taylor, Archer. 1949. "Locutions for 'Never.' " *Romance Philology,* 2:103–134.

Terhune, Kenneth W. 1970. "From National Character to National Behavior: A Reformulation." *Journal of Conflict Resolution,* 14:203–263.

Thiele, Ernst. 1900. *Luthers Sprichwörtersammlung.* Weimar: Herman Böhlaus.

Thompson, Stith. 1955–1958. *Motif-Index of Folk Literature.* 6 vols. Bloomington: Indiana University Press.

Thorner, M. 1909. "Norddeutsche Abortinschriften." *Anthropophyteia Jahrbücher,* 6:437–438.

Trachtenberg, Joshua. 1966. *The Devil and the Jews: The Medieval Conception of the Jew and its Relation to Modern Antisemitism.* New York: Harper Torchbooks.

Vetten, Horst. 1979a. "Die Geschichte des Klo." *Stern,* 47:40–59; 48:192–201; 49:119–131; 50:163–172.

——1983. *Über das Klo: Ein thema, auf das jeder täglich kommt.* Frankfurt, Berlin, Vienna: Ullstein.

Vorberg, Gaston. 1926. "Martin Luthers skatologische Ausdrucksweise und ihre Beziehungen zur Persönlichkeit." *Fortschritte der Sexualwissenschaft und Psychoanalyse,* 2:526–528.

Wackernagel, Wilhelm. 1848. "Die Spottnamen der Völker." *Zeitschrift für Deutsches Alterthum,* 6:254–261.

Wähler, Martin. 1939. "Die Aufgabe der Volkskunde bei der Erforschung des Volkscharakters der europäischen Völker." *Zeitschrift für Volkskunde,* 48:218–227.

Wagner, Richard. 1980. *The Diary of Richard Wagner 1865–1882, The Brown Book.* London: Victor Gollancz.

Waite, Robert G. L. 1977. *The Psychopathic God: Adolf Hitler.* New York: Basic Books.

Waldheim, Dr. von. 1909. "Abtritt-Inschriften aus Langenau in Schlesien." *Anthropophyteia Jahrbücher,* 6:435–436.

——1910. "Abtrittverse und Sprüche aus Preussisch-Schlesien." *Anthropophyteia Jahrbücher,* 7:404–406.

Wander, Karl Friedrich Wilhelm, ed. 1964. *Deutsches Sprichwörter-Lexikon.* 5 vols. Darmstadt: Wissenschaftliche Buchgesellschaft.

Warren, Richard L. 1967. *Education in Rebhausen: A German Village.* New York: Holt, Rinehart and Winston.

Wegeli, Jean. 1912. "Das Gesäss im Völkergedanken: Ein Beitrag zur Gluteralerotik." *Anthropophyteia Jahrbücher,* 9:209–243.

Weibel, Peter. 1970. *Wien: Bildkompendium Wiener Actionismus und Film.* Frankfurt: Kohlkunstverlag.

Wells, F. L. 1951. "Frau Wirtin and Associates: A Note on Alien Corn." *American Imago,* 8:93–97.

Whiting, John W. M. and Irvin L. Child. 1953. *Child Training and Personality: A Cross-Cultural Study.* New Haven: Yale University Press.

Wiesbrock, Heinz. 1957. "Uber Ethnocharakterologie: Wesen, Forschungsprogramm, Methodik." *Kölner Zeitschrift für Soziologie und Sozialpsychologie,* 9:549–586.

Wisdom, J. O. 1966. "What is the Explanatory Theory of Obsessional Neurosis?" *British Journal of Medical Psychology,* 39:335–348.

171

Witte, W. 1975. "The Literary Uses of Obscenity." *German Life & Letters,* 28:360–373.

Wittenwiler, Heinrich. 1956. *Wittenwiler's Ring and the Anonymous Scots Poem Colkelbie Sow: Two Comic-Didactic Works from the Fifteenth Century.* George Fenwick Jones, trans. University of North Carolina Studies in Germanic Languages and Literatures 18. Chapel Hill: University of North Carolina Press.

Wolff, J. 1970–1971. "Rilke's Use of the Word "Rein,' " *German Life & Letters,* 24:144–160.

Wundt, Wilhelm. 1918. *Die Nationen und ihre Philosophie.* Leipzig: Alfred Kröner Verlag.

Wyatt, Frederick and Hans Lukas Teuber. 1944. "German Psychology under the Nazi System: 1933–1940." *Psychological Review,* 51:229–247.

Zglinicki, Friedrich von. 1972. *Kallipygos und Äskulap:* Das Klistier in der Geschichte der Medizin, Kunst und Literatur. Baden-Baden: Verlag für angewandte Wissenschaften.

Zintl, Josef. 1980. "Prosodic Influences on the Meaning of *Leck Mich am Arsch* in Bavarian." *Maledicta,* 4:91–95.

INDEX

174